I0893088

JACK THORNE

Theatre includes: *A Christmas Carol* (The Old Vic, London/Broadway); *The Motive and the Cue* (National Theatre, London/West End); *After Life* (National Theatre); *When Winston Went to War with the Wireless* (Donmar Warehouse, London); *Harry Potter and the Cursed Child* (West End/international); *The Solid Life of Sugar Water* (Graeae/National Theatre/UK tour); *Let the Right One In* (West End/Dundee Rep/Royal Court Theatre, London); *the end of history…* and *Hope* (Royal Court Theatre).

Television includes: *The Hack*; *Adolescence*; *Toxic Town*; *An Almost Christmas Story*; *Best Interests*; *Help*; *Then Barbara Met Alan*; *CripTales*; *The Eddy*; *The Accident*; *His Dark Materials*; *Philip K. Dick's Electric Dreams*; *Kiri*; *This is England* and *National Treasure*.

Film includes: *Joy*; *The Swimmers*; the *Enola Holmes* films; *The Secret Garden* and *Wonder*.

Awards include a Primetime Emmy, an Astra TV Award, five BAFTAs, a Rose d'Or and the 2022 RTS Award for Outstanding Contribution to British Television.

Jack is on the steering group of the TV Access Project, and President of the Writers' Guild of Great Britain.

STEPHEN GRAHAM

Television includes: *This is England '88/88/90*; *Accused*; *Boardwalk Empire*; *Little Boy Blue*; *White House Farm*; *Line of Duty*; *Save Me*; *The Virtues*; *The North Water*; *Time* (also as executive producer); *Help*; *Peaky Blinders*; *A Thousand Blows* (also as executive producer) and *Adolescence* (also as co-creator, co-writer and executive producer).

Film includes: *This is England*; *Public Enemies*; *Pirates of the Caribbean*; *Tinker, Tailor, Solider, Spy*; *Modigliani: Three Days on the Wing of Madness*; *Yardie*; *Journey's End*; *Rocketman*; *The Irishman* (nominated for ten Academy Awards); *Greyhound*; two *Venom* films (*Let There Be Carnage* and *The Last Dance*); *Matilda the Musical*; *Young Woman and the Sea*; *Blitz*; *Deliver Me from Nowhere*; *Peaky Blinders*; *Bunker* and *Ibelin*.

Stephen set up Matriarch Productions alongside his wife, Hannah Walters, in 2019, and they released their first project, the film *Boiling Point*, in 2021. Following the success of the film, Stephen starred in and Matriarch produced its sequel, a five-part drama for the BBC.

Awards include Emmys for Best Supporting Actor, Best Writing in a Limited Series and Best Limited Series for *Adolescence*; the BIFA Richard Harris Award for outstanding services to drama, and an OBE for his services to drama. He has been nominated for seven BAFTA acting awards.

ADOLESCENCE
THE SCRIPTS

JACK THORNE
& STEPHEN GRAHAM

NICK HERN BOOKS
London
www.nickhernbooks.co.uk

Adolescence: The Scripts
first published in Great Britain in 2025
by Nick Hern Books Limited,
The Glasshouse, 49a Goldhawk Road, London W12 8QP

Front cover, left to right: Stephen Graham (as Eddie Miller) and Owen Cooper (as Jamie Miller); back cover, left to right: Ashley Walters (as DI Luke Bascombe), Erin Doherty (as Briony Ariston), Christine Tremarco (as Manda Miller) and Stephen Graham, all courtesy of Netflix © 2024

Designed and typeset by Nick Hern Books, London
Printed and bound in the UK by 4Edge, Essex

A CIP catalogue record for this book is available from the British Library

ISBN 978 1 83904 537 0

Nick Hern Books' authorised representative in the EU is
Easy Access System Europe – Mustamäe tee 50, 10621 Tallinn, Estonia
email gpsr.requests@easproject.com

CONTENTS

JACK THORNE
Co-creator and writer

Adolescence was a train ride no one really expected.

When we made it, we believed in it, and were incredibly proud of it, and then suddenly it turned into this madness.

As Stephen and I said to each other in the middle of it all, we'll never have an experience like this again, and so we'll enjoy every single moment of it.

It started with a phone call. Now, if you've never had a phone call from Stephen Graham before, and I assume most of you haven't, it's quite an experience. It starts with one thought, and then that one thought becomes a thousand thoughts, and then those thousand thoughts sprout legs and run off in all sorts of directions. He has an enthusiasm for the possibility of what drama should be that is entirely infectious.

Stephen had an idea for a show about knife crime. He wanted to do it in four single hours. He wanted to do it with director Phil Barantini. He wanted to do it the way that they had made *Boiling Point*. Each episode in one single shot. He wanted me to write it. I said, 'Why don't we try and write it together?' Stephen had never written anything before, but we had made five shows together (*This is England '86/88/90*, *The Virtues* and *Help*) and we trusted each other, and I thought it could work. He has a brain I want to crawl inside, and he had some trust in me.

It never involved sitting together with laptops; it never involved Stephen typing any words at all. It would start with a phone call where we'd lay out all the pieces of the puzzle, then I'd go away and do some research with Mariella Johnson, who works with me, and call him back with some meat to put on those pieces, at which point it became a butcher's puzzle. We'd talk some more. Then I'd write. And once I was happy with where the script was, I'd share it with him. He'd give some notes, I'd input them, and then I'd send it on to Phil and the producing team. I'd do more notes. Once they were happy, it'd go to Netflix and they'd have thoughts and we'd work on it again. The TV process is one of layers of talking, which is something I love.

The best note Stephen gave to me, and he had to give it a few times, is that the camera doesn't go anywhere without a story. I'd do it all the time – 'The camera travels to find Bascombe doing this or that' – and he'd be like 'No, that'll feel shit.' Do better. And slowly but surely I realised I had to work out the camera path. It rarely ended up being what the camera did, Phil and Matt Lewis, our Director of Photography, are too talented for that to be the case, but it did force me to discover the vocabulary of the one-shot; it forced me to really think about what the snake of the lens can do.

There were two major things that happened during what was a pretty normal writing process. The first came from Mariella. I was struggling with Jamie; something wasn't quite working. Stephen said we can't make this easy and blame it on an alcoholic parent or an abusive uncle, and I agreed, but it meant that Jamie was sort of appearing so unlikely that I didn't think audiences would make the leap. Mariella said you need to look at incel culture. So started a two-year dive into corners of the internet I hadn't appreciated. It changed everything.

The second major thing that happened was that Stephen and I got bored of waiting on an answer as to whether we were greenlit or not. We wrote Episode One and handed it in and then didn't hear anything. It wasn't anyone's fault – the platform we were with then do a legal process before a conventional commissioning process, and that takes quite a long time. Stephen and Phil had a window in the summer of 2024, and we started to get worried when it got to September 2023 that we weren't going to hit that window, so we decided to write Episodes Two and Three on spec. 'On spec' is basically when you are not sure you're going to get paid for something. It's speculative. First episodes are often written this way, second and third episodes rarely. But actually, operating without anyone looking at us was the best thing we could possibly have done. We wanted to make a swing with how the vocabulary of the show worked, and this allowed us to do so.

We were always thinking, always concentrating on Jamie. Who and why he is. Our central conceit was if 'it takes a village to make a child', it also takes a village to destroy one. He isn't the product of the manosphere, he isn't the product of his parenting, he isn't the product of a failing school system, he isn't a product of his friendship group, and he isn't a product of chemicals in his brain. He is a product of *all* these things, and the jagged edges of a one-shot system – that doesn't allow for complete storytelling – that emphasises the partial – meant that we tumbled through his life looking for some questions, without ever answering. As such, to me, it felt a lot like theatre. Where you tell some answers on stage, and rely on the audience to give it an offstage life.

The process of filming also had lots of similarities with theatre. Phil's brilliant system for making the show was first a week of rehearsal with just the cast and me and Matt, then week two was the technical rehearsal, when everyone else came in, and week three was the shoot week, when we'd shoot the episode once in the morning, and once in the afternoon. Phil creates a kind and happy set, and that first week, being given the opportunity for the actors and me to work through their lines, was just beautiful. It also gave me a window into what he and Matt had to do.

We shot Episode Three first, and in so many ways that was the best proof of how a one-shot could work. Conventionally you'd shoot a conversation like that with one take on one side of it, facing one of the characters, one take on the other side, on the other character, and then multiple takes covering both of them. With our one-take approach, the camera couldn't catch every line without it swinging back and forth, whizzing between faces like a giddying tennis match. So Phil and Matt would talk for ages over which bits of the conversation would be given to which face. It was amazing to see. At the same time, I watched a combination of Phil and the wonderful Erin Doherty slowly bring Owen Cooper into full bloom. What a wonderful Jamie, what a wonderful cast.

A TV show is not written by a writer, but authored by everyone that works on it. Stephen and I are so grateful to Toby Bentley, Mona Qureshi, Anne Mensah, Ted Sarandos and Bela Bajaria. We are so grateful to Mark Herbert, Emily Feller, Niall Shamma, Peter Balm and everyone at Warp. We are so grateful to Brad Pitt, Dede Gardner, Jeremy Kleiner, Nina Wolarsky and Carina Sposato, and everyone at Plan B. We are so grateful to Hannah Walters and Matriarch. We are so grateful to our producer Jo Johnson, who held us all together through those months of filming, and lived on a yoga farm during it to cope with the stress of it. We are so grateful to all the cast. We are so grateful to all the crew.

We are very proud of what we made, it was an incredible thing to be part of. The summer of 2024 was a beautiful summer and in a little town called Pontefract, outside of Rotherham, we were given the freedom to do something a bit weird. The best responses I've had about the project are phone calls or e-mails from old school friends saying they'd just had a conversation that they'd never had before. I grew up watching TV on the sofa with my mum and my sister, talking about what we'd seen. TV is an empathy box; sitting in the corner of the room, it reaches into a conversation. I am so pleased this provoked some.

STEPHEN GRAHAM
Co-creator, writer and actor

As is always the case, I couldn't have put it any better than what Jack has written, but I would just like to add that in my humble opinion there is no one else who could have penned this unique project quite like Jack… and I would like to thank him from the bottom of my heart – for his patience, his kindness and his humility – in helping me realise this wonderful thing which started as a very passionate idea inside of my head.

May we all keep tapping into the consciousness of ideas that can create conversation and allow us to find love and empathy and hope.

The children are our future. We are merely borrowing the world from them.

Loads a love… Namaste.

Philip Barantini and Stephen Graham, courtesy of Netflix © 2024

PHILIP BARANTINI
Director

After making the BBC TV miniseries *Boiling Point*, which was released in 2023, I was eager for my next project to be something different. I didn't know what exactly, but I wanted it to be a challenge. For me, the challenge is what makes any project fun. Little did I know that a video call with production company Plan B Entertainment was about to offer up exactly what I'd been looking for…

The initial brief was essentially a blank canvas in terms of subject matter and form. I desperately wanted to work again with my *Boiling Point* collaborator Stephen Graham, one of my closest friends for over twenty years. Having built up such a close understanding, I instinctively knew that whatever the project, we would be able to craft something unique, with its own clear identity, much as we had with *Boiling Point.* We spoke at length about our mutual love for the Channel 4 docuseries *24 Hours in Police Custody*, which keeps the action confined within a police station. In that series, you get to see the full gamut of a police officer's job, from dealing with the initial arrest, through processing the suspect, to handing them over to the next stage of the criminal justice system.

Stephen had been ruminating on an article he had read on the recent increase in teenage-on-teenage murders, specifically young boys and knife crime. With this subject matter, we knew that there was something tangible and contemporary we could make, which could transfer to the screen in a visceral, character-led way. Stephen reached out to his regular collaborator Jack Thorne to write the scripts, but Jack told Stephen he'd love to co-write it with him. The pair soon returned with a story which, from their initial pitch, hit me right in the guts. As the father of a young child myself, I felt there was an extraordinary urgency and truth to this story, and that I needed to tell it.

The next stage was to establish what the series would be like visually. Having already laid down something of a visual style with *Boiling Point*, realism felt like the right approach here: with such weighty subject matter, it would be important not to go over the top stylistically. The priority would be to capture the performances, and to keep the audience locked into the scenario, keeping them hooked as the layers of the story are revealed.

It became clear to me and my cinematographer, Matthew Lewis, that our work on *Boiling Point* would be pushed to the next level here. Each episode would be shot in real time, in a different location, in a single take. Achieving this required an intricate balance: a camera that moves with the restless energy of youth; performances that feel unfiltered and lived-in; and a visual language that evolves alongside the characters. We would aim to create a world in which the actors are immersed in their characters within a real-world setting; where they would drive the story and dictate where the camera should be, as opposed to having the camera dictate to the actors. It was vital that the series should have a fluid feel and a lightness of touch, to let the story breathe and bring the audience in as an observer – at times almost a participant – whilst never overpowering the narrative.

Working with Jack and Stephen, we planned how the locations could be used very simply and naturally to progress the story on a visual level. The opening episode would stay with the family in a whirlwind of confusion, getting to the bottom of what's going on. Then in Episode Two the story would open up, showing the impact of the crime on Jamie's schoolmates, teachers and, crucially, the law enforcement officers who are investigating the case. We would begin to dig into the reason why this has happened – and why it *is* happening – unearthing a much deeper malaise amongst the younger generation as the series progresses. The confrontational Episode Three would delve into Jamie's psyche, letting the audience glimpse his repressed rage as it eventually boils over; but also showing how the psychologist is tested, how rattled she is when she discovers the truly shocking nature of the situation. Our final episode – whilst not depicting Jamie on screen – leaves his shadow very much hanging over his family. We see them a few months down the line, the family unit deeply fractured, but striving to come to terms with their new reality, as well as their own baffled sense of guilt and responsibility for their son's actions.

Coming from an acting background myself, I knew that to properly immerse the audience in the world of this story, to keep it as grounded as possible, it was necessary for Jamie to be played by an unknown young actor. Having established performers in the cast too – such as Stephen as Jamie's father, and Ashley Walters as DI Luke Bascombe – would really help: their supportive presence, both on and off camera, would give the younger actors something to play off, help them to feel their characters come alive in their own organic way. My role as director was to create the strongest possible sense of trust between the performers and the technical crew: they would all be working so closely together throughout the shoot, almost intertwined. Both sides would need the space to breathe, and the freedom to explore moments of spontaneity in order to get to the truth of the project.

Another of my key processes as a director is to allow the actors to build up their own characters in their world, and to be willing to stray from the script at times, be that through dialogue or through action. One of the most notable moments of improvisation occurs in Episode Three, when Owen Cooper (playing Jamie) gives a yawn. It was completely accidental, but Erin Doherty (playing the psychologist) used it as a springboard to add dialogue – and from there we get more of a character insight: Jamie's nonchalance and his irritation at having to be there; and on the other side, the psychologist asserting her authority.

Moments like these, however, would not have been possible were it not for the extensive rehearsal time – both for the actors, but also for the technical crew. Each episode was given a three-week block in the schedule: the first week was a rehearsal for the actors, where we would break down and then run through each episode, with the crew also establishing a running order of the blocking of the episode and what was needed where and when. The second week would be the technical rehearsal in which we would essentially dry-run the shooting of the episode. This was crucial in ironing out any issues, both technically and from a performance perspective, as it was here that the two would intertwine for the first time on set. The final week would be the official shoot.

With each episode running at around sixty minutes, we would run through each episode twice for five days of the shoot. This would leave us with ten takes in total, which helped in dialling up the focus of everyone involved, whilst also making the days much more structured and ultimately achievable. We were able to find a flow which didn't wear out our cast and crew, whilst also being able to see the full episode after one day, with time to make any tweaks or suggestions the following day.

Post-production was where the eight-month process crystallised. The episodes were essentially locked – due to them each being a single, unaltered take – so the next stage was intensifying the emotional heft where possible, through sound design and score. Collaborating with my regular composers, David Ridley and Aaron May, we leaned into the emotive narrative beats and the sense of loss: both of life, and also of innocence. The choral soundscape being sung by children emphasised that sense of innocence with regards to the victim of Jamie's attack. I also had the idea to invite Emilia Holliday (who played Katie in the series) to sing as part of the score, breaking the wall between realities and further enveloping the audience on an almost meta level.

At the time we were making *Adolescence*, we didn't anticipate that it would become such a talked-about, globally recognised show. We knew that the story we were telling was important and current, and that we were exploring a scarily relevant and seemingly growing trend. Our first priority was to make an effective drama, one where those urgent issues would have a viable and tangible grounding.

Directing *Adolescence* was about much more than telling a story; it was about crafting an experience that stays with the audience long after the credits roll. It was a test of stamina, precision and instinct. It has been the most challenging and rewarding eight months of my career to date.

JAMES BLOODWORTH

Insecurity has long been central to the business models of certain industries. Markets don't simply cater to existing needs but must also create them. The female beauty industry is a case in point. Popular concepts of femininity are bound up with the acquisition of certain consumer items such as make-up, hair products, fillers or more extreme surgical interventions. The UK cosmetics market is estimated to be worth between £8 to 11 billion annually.

One way to understand the manosphere – an array of male-supremacist subcultures that have emerged online in recent decades – is to see it in the context of this insecurity industrial complex. Powered by social media, masculinity entrepreneurs including the malignant influencer Andrew Tate have created multi-million-pound businesses by convincing young men that there is something wrong with them.

The manosphere is a misogynistic online underworld populated by the predatory and the pitiful; but it is also a sales funnel, a giant shakedown that preys on insecurity. This was touched on in *Adolescence*. During a conversation with the clinical psychologist, Jamie, the teenage protagonist who murders a girl from his school, briefly mentions the 'eighty-twenty' rule, a manosphere concept. 'Eighty per cent of women are attracted to twenty per cent of men.' In a different episode, another teenager explains it further: 'You must trick them, because you'll never get them in a normal way.'

The eighty-twenty rule (sometimes called the Pareto Principle) is the idea that, thanks to feminism and the sexual revolution, a majority of men are destined to end up frustrated and alone. If feminism has denied men their birthright, then the manosphere is intent on wrestling it back. While I was researching my book about the manosphere, I heard one *soi-disant* masculinity guru – who was running his own $10,000 'alpha male' bootcamp in the Nevada desert – put it as follows:

> As we got into monogamous societies, what happened was low-status men got at least one girl that they could have sex with. Then after birth control and the sexual revolution we allowed people to choose more, and what women were choosing was the high-status men, so these men at the bottom became surplus again. That's why you guys are here.

In other words, women's liberation has rendered the majority of the male species superfluous. Meanwhile sex and companionship are being monopolised by a small elite.

Fear is the white wallpaper of the manosphere. Fear of obsolescence; fear of being perpetually single; fear of failing to perform adequately in the bedroom; of being cheated on by a woman; of unknowingly raising another man's child (cuckoldry). Fear of false rape accusations. Fear of losing (or never gaining) the respect of other men. Even ostensibly serious and sober masculinity influencers like the Canadian psychology professor Jordan Peterson have been known to talk in the same histrionic register. 'Women pick a monogamous marriage and they cheat with high-status guys,' he told Joe Rogan's podcast in 2018.

Fear is also a reliable way of converting leads (in this case, audiences of men watching manosphere content on platforms such as YouTube and TikTok) into paying customers. Conspiracy theories like the eighty-twenty rule are enthusiastically propagated by those who stand to profit from the fear and cynicism such ideas generate. A thousand online content mills soften you up with a similar message: it's eighty-twenty out there, the law of the jungle – there is no common humanity, just winners and losers. Then the masculinity hucksters swoop in for the shakedown. By punching your credit card details into a website and buying a course, you too can avoid the fate of the surplus men.

Teenagers and young adults are particularly susceptible to this kind of emotional blackmail. This is a time in one's life when insecurity sits at the table uninvited, dressed in a variety of outfits. I speak from experience: I too was susceptible to the snake oil. In 2006 I attended a pick-up artist bootcamp in London. I was twenty-three at the time and at least half-believed the gurus who claimed they could fix my romantic woes with scripts and gambits (and by taking my money).

A few months after the bootcamp I stopped visiting the pick-up forums and went back to my old life again. I decided that I didn't need that stuff after all. Snake-oil salesmen be damned. But the architecture of the internet was radically different back then. There was no infinite scroll or never-ending feed; no algorithm engineered to exploit every human vulnerability and pull a person deeper into the void. The two worlds (online and offline) were more distinct than they are today.

These days the flattening, utopian drive towards connection has been supplanted by the algorithmic internet: an online world that is saturated with the logic of late-stage capitalism. The social media entrepreneurs of today generate clicks and cash not by promoting connection, but by selling their followers bespoke versions of reality. The prevailing culture is one of stratification and social comparison. The more beauty and abundance on one side of the screen, the greater the sense of material and spiritual impoverishment on the other. You aren't supposed to feel good enough. If you did, you might never buy anything.

If social media has created a looking-glass world, manosphere influencers have become adept at using it to captivate adolescent men. Telegenic charisma has become the most valuable social commodity of all, a force multiplier on a par with outrage and spectacle. Honesty stands little chance against untruths arrestingly put.

Along with charisma and a rigid code of unreconstructed masculinity, they use it to promote a succession of perfect images. Content is filmed against a glittering and ostentatious backdrop: a world of fast cars, enormous mansions and private jets. The most important status symbol of all is semi-clothed women who function as party prettifiers and commodities. It is a *mise en scène* designed to elicit feelings of inferiority. The message is that this is how the twenty per cent – the 'chads', the alphas, the high-status males – live.

Of course, even the lifestyle is rarely what it seems. As part of their course in Las Vegas, the students were taken out to the Nevada desert for photoshoots next to rented Lamborghinis. 'When you have a solid social media profile, you're showing huge evolutionary signs that you're a high-status male,' their course leader told them. Those who do acquire wealth usually do so thanks to their ability to extract money from a Pied Piper-like following. They hammer away at young men's insecurities before presenting themselves as saviours and guides: 'You are poor and weak; women will laugh at you; other men won't respect you. Now buy my course for £49.95 a month or stay at home, rotting in your bedroom.'

This is how the manosphere gets you: staring into the luminescent glass rectangle, primed and ready for the next flamboyant sales pitch. It's how the insecurity industrial complex remakes itself for a new generation.

James Bloodworth is the author of Lost Boys: A Personal Journey Through the Manosphere (*Atlantic Books, 2025*).

SUSIE McDONALD

When my charity Tender was approached by Netflix to preview their upcoming drama series *Adolescence*, it was because the show's creators, Jack Thorne and Stephen Graham, felt that it could have a wider social impact than most television shows. They thought there might be an educational angle that could be used to open up conversations about the issues it raises. Well, they weren't wrong!

I was given a heads-up by the Netflix team about the storyline: a young boy is accused of murdering a girl from his school. As I watched the first episode – which begins with the police battering down the door of a family home and making their way into the bedroom of a small boy, who is so frightened by this that he wets himself – I already knew that this drama was going to make a difference. I knew perfectly well that the boy could be guilty of the crime – that, despite his age and appearance, he could be capable of committing a terrible act of violence. And I sensed that this would be the drama that could make society realise, at last, that we must protect our boys from becoming the perpetrators of these horrifying acts.

Watching this boy calling for his dad – his voice not yet broken, his bedroom decorated with childish spaceships – I began to cry. I knew how badly we've been letting down our boys. And, by doing so, letting down our girls too.

I knew this because of the work that Tender has been doing for the last twenty years. Through our programmes in schools and youth centres across the country, we prevent domestic and sexual violence by equipping children and young people with the skills to navigate healthy relationships and identify the early warning signs of abusive behaviours. Over the last five years, we've seen a steady but significant increase in misogynistic – and sometimes extreme – attitudes amongst young men. Some believe they are being manipulated by girls and are losing their masculinity. Some (as young as ten years old) talk about strangulation as part of a sexual relationship. And you can clearly see from news reports that cases of teenage boys killing, or attempting to kill, teenage girls are happening and not a work of fiction.

Society has tended to focus its attention on the vulnerability of girls and women – on the need to protect them from the dangers of domestic and sexual violence, from strangers in public spaces, and even from husbands and lovers. What *Adolescence* has done is to broaden the focus to include the importance of protecting boys from becoming capable of committing acts of violence against girls. This is not about punishing boys, but about preventing them from becoming the next generation of domestic abuse perpetrators. By equipping them with skills and knowledge, we can enable them to become the best versions of themselves. Every day in our work at Tender, we see boys desperate to be kind, strong and loving. But, as author Tim Winton says:

> Boys and young men are so routinely expected to betray their better natures, to smother their consciences, to renounce the best of themselves and submit to something low and mean. As if there's only one way of being a bloke, one valid interpretation of the part, the role, if you like. There's a constant pressure to enlist, to pull on the uniform of misogyny and join the Shithead Army that enforces and polices sexism.

I have long felt that, in order to tackle the violence that women and girls experience, we need to focus more on engaging boys and men. At Tender, their inclusion in our work promoting healthy relationships isn't simply welcome; it's vital. They are entitled to this education. But men and boys can feel uncomfortable about exploring these issues, or worried about being viewed as the problem, and this can sometimes lead to them withdrawing altogether. We've always known how vital it is that our programmes see people as the solution, not as the problem.

I fed back to Netflix how powerful and important I thought this drama was. Then, a couple of weeks before *Adolescence* premiered, Netflix and Tender co-hosted a private screening for professionals from the domestic abuse and youth violence sectors, followed by a Q&A with Jack, Stephen and Jo Johnson, the show's producer. There were a couple of government special advisors and a senior politician in the room too. The response from the audience was powerful and positive.

Prime Minister Keir Starmer was reported to have watched the series with his teenage children, and felt strongly that schools should be given free access to view the series. Teachers can now access it, free of charge, through the charity Into Film. Tender was asked by Netflix to create education resource packs for teachers and for parents/families. Designed for secondary schools, the teaching resource provides a guide to the language and tactics of harmful online content, focusing on key themes such as stereotypes, misogyny and personal values. The main objective of these lessons is to enable all students to feel empowered to make positive choices. The parent/carer resource provides practical advice on discussing these issues with young people, with suggestions on how to help them navigate social media safely.

Tender was invited to take part in a roundtable event at 10 Downing Street, alongside other charities and the makers of *Adolescence*, to discuss the issues and possible solutions. I was pleased to be there, but made the point that a drama series, on its own, wasn't enough to solve the challenge of men's violence against women. To properly prevent it, we need to equip children with the skills to build relationships that are healthy, kind and equal. Children must be clear about their rights to have healthy relationships, but also to their responsibility to treat others with respect. Relationship education must be delivered by skilled, fully trained specialist teachers, or schools must be given budgets to enable them to partner with specialist organisations.

Sadly, as a result of Tender's name being associated with the series, we received some pretty nasty online communications from bad-faith individuals who couldn't, or simply wouldn't, understand that we want *all* children to be safe and protected. Many of them accused us of hating men, which couldn't be further from the truth.

I understand the power of drama and storytelling to reach audiences in a way that a documentary or personal appeal generally can't. In our work, we use scripts, characters and scenarios to explore experiences and ideas from a safe distance. And we use drama techniques to create opportunities to play, to imagine, and to rehearse responses to situations that young people might face as they grow up.

Our programmes equip young people with language to discuss and challenge misogyny and discrimination, and to identify and call out inappropriate behaviour. We explore what this looks like in both the 'real world' and online. And we see a tangible impact: boys now openly challenge sexism amongst their peers at school; teachers report positive changes in children; and parents feel more prepared to speak to their children about what they are seeing online.

But drama can let us down too. We've become so familiar with images and depictions of women as victims – dead in ditches, in lockups, in dark cellars – that we are perhaps desensitised to them. We've come to expect a focus on the trauma of the victim's family. We rarely see the impact of violence on the families of the perpetrator: how they experience guilt and bereavement, and often suffer reprisals. *Adolescence* enables us to consider the ripple effect of violence in a way that is both rare and hugely valuable.

One of the most important moments in *Adolescence* (spoiler alert!) is when Jamie says he will plead guilty. For me, this is a moment of hope. It leaves no room for conspiracy theorists – or for those still hoping for a last-minute plot twist that lets him off the hook and proves he hasn't committed this appalling crime. Crime dramas perhaps have a responsibility to confront the implications of the crimes they depict, and to ensure that their fictional perpetrators are held properly accountable: no excuses, no suggestion that the victim deserved it, and no vindicating backstory of trauma.

Stephen Graham wanted Jamie to come from a loving and stable home, one without a history of violence or alcohol abuse. There are no easy explanations. But perhaps, if we are parents ourselves, we need to consider our accountability too. What is good parenting? Is it enough just to avoid being a violent drunk? To paraphrase Tiernan Brady, who campaigns for social inclusion, good parenting isn't simply the absence of bad parenting. Have we all just been keeping our fingers crossed that we could keep our children safe? Can we do that simply by restricting and tracking their movements? How do we know that, as we strive to protect them in the real world, they won't get lost in the online one?

'He was in his bedroom. We thought he was safe,' say the parents in *Adolescence*. Nothing could be further from the truth.

Susie McDonald MBE is the CEO of Tender (tender.org.uk).

A NOTE ON THE SCRIPTS
Jack Thorne & Stephen Graham

The scripts in this book are the versions we went into rehearsal with.

They then changed as the show was built with our amazing cast.

The show became theirs and it changed to fit them.

It felt more interesting to show you where we started than where we got to. (You can still watch that.)

EPISODE ONE

Jon Furlong (as Derek) and Owen Cooper (as Jamie Miller), courtesy of Netflix © 2024

EXT. INDUSTRIAL ESTATE

DI BASCOMBE, forties, is eating an apple.

A text arrives. He looks at his phone. ADAM - *'I've got that bad belly again. Do I have to go to school?'* It comes complete with a vomit emoji. The eagle-eyed will pick out the time, 6.13 a.m.

He crunches his face in a frown.

He eats the core of the apple, he throws away the stem.

Behind him we pick out two police vans and an unmarked Volvo.

INT. POLICE CAR

DI BASCOMBE gets into the Volvo. He winces.

DS FRANK, thirties, looks across at him.

DS FRANK
You okay?

DI BASCOMBE
I think apples are not good for my stomach acid or something...

DS FRANK
So why - eat them?

DI BASCOMBE
Tracy's idea. Instead of cigs. I'm getting through six a day.

DS FRANK
The full bushel.

DI BASCOMBE laughs. His phone buzzes again. He looks at it, it says: *'Dad?'*

DI BASCOMBE

Adam.

He shows her his phone.

DS FRANK

Six a.m. texts? That's commitment. He really doesn't want to go to school.

DI BASCOMBE

No, he just knows Tracy'll say no, I'm the soft touch.

DS FRANK

What you gonna reply?

DI BASCOMBE

She'll sort it. He'll go.

DS FRANK smiles.

DI BASCOMBE (CONT'D)

Know thyself.

DI BASCOMBE lets out a burp.

DS FRANK

Disgusting.

The radio comes through.

RADIO (SGT PETE PHILLIPS) (O.S)

Bravo Delta four zero to Bravo Delta five zero, are you receiving, over?

DI BASCOMBE

Hi Pete.

RADIO (SGT PETE PHILLIPS)(O.S)

Confirming Ten-Fifty-One. Ready to go. Over.

DI BASCOMBE checks the time. He flicks a button on the radio.

DI BASCOMBE
Bravo Delta five zero to Bravo Delta six zero, you ready to roll out?

RADIO (TONIA SIMPSON)(O.S)
Yes yes.

DI BASCOMBE
DI Bascombe received.

DI BASCOMBE flicks over the radio again.

DI BASCOMBE
Pete. Let's go. Over.

He nods at DS FRANK, who takes a deep breath.

The vans go first. They watch them go.

They turn on the ignition and follow, close behind. Closer than most cars follow.

They go slow, and quiet, so as not to alert anyone.

A slug of a cavalcade, turning left and then right into a small residential street.

EXT. 24 BURGHLEY ROAD, THE MILLER HOUSE

They park up in the middle of the street and are fast out of the cars.

The vans in front spill out armed police officers, the ARMED RESPONSE UNIT, DI BASCOMBE and DS FRANK hold back but switch on their body cams.

The armed officers move swiftly to number 24.

A RED DOOR ENFORCER is brought through the phalanx, carried by two men.

With a nod from DI BASCOMBE it is used to SMASH the door in.

The two officers on the RED DOOR ENFORCER then stand to the side to allow the other officers - eight of them - to spill into the house.

INT. HALLWAY. 24 BURGHLEY ROAD, THE MILLER HOUSE

EDDIE flies down the stairs.

EDDIE
What the fuck -

OFFICER
ARMED POLICE. HANDS ON YOUR HEAD.

EDDIE
I haven't done anything. Whatever you think you're here for - you've made a mistake -

OFFICER
Against the wall. Now.

The other police officers are past him and up the stairs. We turn into the kitchen.

INT. KITCHEN. 24 BURGHLEY ROAD. THE MILLER HOUSE

And we see MANDA being put on the floor. She has wet hair and is in a dressing gown.

MANDA
What is this?

INT. HALLWAY. 24 BURGHLEY ROAD. THE MILLER HOUSE

We reverse out with an officer, and turn to see DI BASCOMBE and DS FRANK enter the house. DI BASCOMBE stops by EDDIE.

DI BASCOMBE
My name is Detective Inspector Bascombe. I'm with the South Yorkshire Police. This is a warrant for the search of your home, do you understand?

EDDIE
What you doing here? What you doing?

Two CSI OFFICERS are coming through into the house.

EDDIE (CONT'D)
I don't understand any of this. Why you here?

The CSI OFFICERS peel off in one of two directions. DI BASCOMBE follows them up the stairs.

TWO ARMED OFFICERS are standing outside a door, with a nod from DI BASCOMBE they open the door.

INT. JAMIE'S BEDROOM. THE MILLER HOUSE

To reveal - JAMIE, thirteen years old - sitting in bed, aware of the commotion, looking really really scared.

OFFICER
POLICE. ON THE FLOOR. ON THE FLOOR.

DI BASCOMBE
Jamie Miller, the time is oh-six seventeen, I am arresting you on suspicion of -

EDDIE
What do you think he's done?

EDDIE has somehow made it up to the room.

DI BASCOMBE
Get him out of the room.

An officer is fast at EDDIE and is shepherding him out of the room.

EDDIE
Whatever you think he's done he hasn't –

EDDIE pushes back. The OFFICER keeps firm hold but they're locked.

EDDIE (CONT'D)
Jamie's a good boy.

We look back at the terrified JAMIE and then spin back to his dad.

DI BASCOMBE
Mr Miller. I will arrest you for obstruction.

EDDIE
He's my son. HE'S MY SON.

He makes to push forward once more. Another OFFICER comes at him with a taser (though it's not pointed at him, there is a sense of threat).

OFFICER
On the floor. Now.

EDDIE reverses out into the hall where he gets on the floor.

EDDIE
You're okay, Jamie. You're okay.

JAMIE
Dad.

We look for a moment at the photos on the wall above him.

Family photos of Eddie, Jamie, Manda and Lisa. Them on holiday wearing stupid sunglasses. Jamie with a football at his feet. Lisa on a new bike.

EDDIE
You're okay. I'm okay. YOU'RE OKAY.

DI BASCOMBE
Jamie Miller, the time is oh-six seventeen. I am arresting you on suspicion of murder. You do not have to say anything. But, it may harm your defence if you do not mention when questioned something which you later rely on in court. Anything you do say may be given in evidence. Do you understand, Jamie? Do you understand?

JAMIE
I HAVEN'T DONE ANYTHING, Dad. I haven't.

DI BASCOMBE
Jamie. I need you to say you've understood.

JAMIE
Dad?

EDDIE
Tell him you understand, and then we can get this cleared up, yeah?

JAMIE
I understand. I UNDERSTAND.

We close on JAMIE's panicked face. A tear rolls down it.

DI BASCOMBE
Okay. We're going to get you on your feet now. Have you got anything in your pockets which could prick me or yourself or otherwise cause harm, Jamie?

JAMIE
No.

JAMIE is pulled up to his feet. We see a piss stain clearly down his pyjama bottoms. BASCOMBE notices it and his demeanour shifts slightly.

DI BASCOMBE
You want to change your trousers, son?

JAMIE
Yes.

DI BASCOMBE
Want me to get your dad?

JAMIE
Yes please.

DI BASCOMBE
Don't move.

DI BASCOMBE heads out to the landing to find EDDIE, still under supervision of armed officers.

DI BASCOMBE (CONT'D)
Stand down please. Mr Miller, come in, he's had an accident. You need to help him, please.

EDDIE darts past LISA, seventeen years old, lying on the ground -

She's sobbing, she doesn't know what's going on.

EDDIE
Lisa. You're okay. You're okay darling.

LISA
Dad...

EDDIE
Just a mistake.

- and into Jamie's room.

EDDIE (CONT'D)
Jay?

INT. THE MILLER HOUSE

The camera rolls to TONIA as she enters the parents' bedroom.

TONIA SIMPSON
Is this the parents' room?

She picks up a wicker laundry basket and empties its contents into a large forensics bag.

She moves on to the wardrobe.

She pulls all the clothes out and lays them carefully on the bed piece by piece, then searches down the front and back of the inside of the wardrobe. She's being absolutely methodical.

DI BASCOMBE leads JAMIE and EDDIE out of Jamie's room.

DI BASCOMBE
You don't need your trainers, I've got slippers for you downstairs.

EDDIE
Can I come with you?

DI BASCOMBE
You're going to have to wait till we leave, you can follow us once we have him in the van.

EDDIE turns to LISA.

EDDIE
Go and get your mum, you're okay.

Then he spots TONIA in his bedroom.

EDDIE (CONT'D)
Excuse me, what you doing with my dirty pants?

TONIA
It's evidence I'm afraid. You'll get them back.

EDDIE
There's nothing in there!

He heads down the stairs and sees MANDA pushing off an officer to get outside to JAMIE.

The other CSI is emptying the dishwasher of all the knives.

EDDIE (CONT'D)
What are you doing? Just tell me what you're looking for. You're wrecking the house!

EDDIE tries to follow them out to the van.

EXT. BURGHLEY ROAD

DS FRANK is fast after them, and stops them before they can get any closer.

DS FRANK
Mr Miller? Mr Miller. Two things I need to say to you, okay? Your head straight?

EDDIE
No.

MANDA
What happened here?

DS FRANK
Your son has been arrested on suspicion of murder. We are taking him for questioning. You can follow us to the station, we're on Heywood Street.

EDDIE
He's a kid. He didn't do that.

MANDA
He couldn't.

DS FRANK hands him a form.

MANDA (CONT'D)
Why do you need guns for a thirteen-year-old?

DS FRANK
The second thing is, and this isn't the time for it, but I need to give it you. You might be entitled to compensation for any mess we made today. Fill this in. Get it back to us.

EDDIE
He didn't do anything. Not my boy. He didn't do anything.

DS FRANK
Do you understand what I said to you?

EDDIE takes a step towards DS FRANK. His aggression flowering for a moment.

EDDIE
Do you understand what I said to you? I hope you're happy with yourselves.

MANDA
Eddie.

He pulls back instantly.

DS FRANK
I'm going to go now. I'll see you at the station.

EDDIE nods. MANDA looks at him.

The street has lots of people on it now, neighbours watching what's happening, trying to work out what's going on.

We see the ARMED RESPONSE UNIT getting in the vans.

INT. POLICE VAN

DS FRANK heads towards her car, but we swerve into a van, where JAMIE is loaded into a caged section at the back. The cage is shut and locked. JAMIE looks at it, shocked.

DI BASCOMBE sits on a seat facing the caged area. Beside him, already inside, is a social worker, DEREK.

DI BASCOMBE
Base, this is Bravo Delta five zero.

BASE (O.S.)
Go ahead.

DI BASCOMBE
Ten-ninety-five, all okay and cooperative.

BASE (O.S.)
Received, over.

DI BASCOMBE turns and signals the driver, who starts the van.

We travel inside it.

Looking at JAMIE.

Who sits there numbly.

He doesn't know how to feel. He doesn't know what just happened. We see his vulnerability and fear.

We wait for thirty seconds.

We wait for a minute.

Just studying his face.

JAMIE
I didn't do anything. I didn't do anything.

DI BASCOMBE
We'll talk some more when we get to the station.

JAMIE
But you've made a mistake.

DI BASCOMBE
Before you say anything more to me. These are serious charges, and I think we should be in the interview room before we talk too much more about them. I also think you should get a lawyer, we have one on duty, or your parents can find one of your own, talk to them, it doesn't make you seem

more guilty, it just protects your interests, okay?

JAMIE
You've made a big mistake.

DI BASCOMBE
Okay, son. Okay.

JAMIE starts to cry.

We just watch him.

Crying.

We're travelling through the streets of the city, and we're watching JAMIE's face.

DI BASCOMBE (CONT'D)
One thing you should be thinking about, this is Derek, for the purpose of your arrest he's your appropriate adult –

DEREK
Hello Jamie. I'm from Doncaster social services.

DI BASCOMBE
The custody sergeant is going to ask you if you want to keep Derek here on, or whether you want to choose someone else, or whether you want a parent with you. This will be for all searches, for discussing anything with your lawyer, and –

JAMIE
What will you need to search?

DI BASCOMBE
– and for the interview. Again, nothing will prejudice your case, whatever you decide.

JAMIE
I want my dad.

DI BASCOMBE
You will be talking to -

JAMIE
(to DEREK)
No offence.

DI BASCOMBE
You will be talking to the custody sergeant about that, I just wanted to give you the chance to think about it.

We look across to DI BASCOMBE, whose face looks grey with anxiety and worry. He doesn't want to screw this up.

He looks at JAMIE, trying to work out what the lad is thinking.

Then he looks forward again.

We see DI BASCOMBE force out all casual thoughts.

His back grows as he becomes more rigid in his brain.

JAMIE
I don't even know who I'm supposed to've done anything to.

DEREK
The inspector's right, Jamie, you should just wait.

JAMIE
I don't even know anything.

DI BASCOMBE
Okay. Enough now. Let's talk about this later.

And we do, we wait.

As the tears dry on JAMIE's face.

He tries to look back to see who's following them.

He doesn't see anything or anyone.

He looks forward.

He grinds his teeth.

INT. CUSTODY VEHICLE DOCK. HEYWOOD STREET POLICE STATION

They pull up into the custody dock.

DI BASCOMBE undoes the cage and helps JAMIE from the van. DEREK follows.

They lead JAMIE to a side door, DI BASCOMBE hits the intercom.

SGT GOLDING (O.S.)
Custody desk.

DI BASCOMBE
DI Bascombe, one in custody.

The door buzzes open.

DI BASCOMBE (CONT'D)
Inside please.

DI BASCOMBE follows JAMIE and DEREK through into a holding unit. He buzzes the bell, and the second door opens.

INT. CUSTODY SUITE. HEYWOOD STREET POLICE STATION

DI BASCOMBE leads JAMIE to the custody desks, and presents him to SGT GOLDING, early fifties, entirely comfortable in his job. DI BASCOMBE hands

SGT GOLDING a piece of paper, which SGT GOLDING reads over.

DI BASCOMBE
This is Jamie. He's thirteen. He's been arrested on suspicion of murder.

SGT GOLDING
Okay Jamie. Can you tell me your full name please, son?

JAMIE
I didn't do it.

SGT GOLDING
That's not to do with me - just answer my questions please, Jamie.

JAMIE
Jamie Edward Miller.

We close on his glassy eyes.

SGT GOLDING
Have you had your rights explained to you, Jamie?

JAMIE
What?

SGT GOLDING
Did the officer explain that you don't need to speak, but anything you do say may be given in evidence?

JAMIE
Yeah.

SGT GOLDING
Will you be wanting a lawyer?

JAMIE

Yes.

SGT GOLDING

Do you have a lawyer or do you want the station to supply one?

JAMIE

I don't know. I don't think we do. Can you ask my dad?

SGT GOLDING

Yes. Because you are a juvenile you will need to be supported by an appropriate adult, would you like that to be one of your parents, or would you like that be Derek, or someone else we can supply?

JAMIE

I'd like my dad please.

SGT GOLDING

If you'd like to think further...

JAMIE

My dad. Please.

SGT GOLDING

Okay. Next business: are you fit and well?

JAMIE

What?

SGT GOLDING

Are you currently taking any medication?

JAMIE

No.

SGT GOLDING
Do you have any long-term medical conditions such as asthma or any serious allergies?

JAMIE
No.

SGT GOLDING
Have you ever attempted to take your life or self-harmed?

JAMIE
No.

SGT GOLDING
Have you had breakfast, son?

JAMIE
No.

SGT GOLDING
Okay Jamie. I am – it's six thirty-one – authorising your detention so the officers can preserve evidence by questioning you about the offence you are suspected of. You can be held at this police station for twenty-four hours. Your detention here will be reviewed by an independent inspector on a regular basis and you, your solicitor or your appropriate adult will be able to make representations about your detention at that review, have you understood all that?

JAMIE
Yeah.

SGT GOLDING
Great, let's get you to a cell - it'll be just you in there - and then we'll fetch you some breakfast. Think we've got some cornflakes, that okay?

JAMIE
Yeah.

EDDIE, LISA and MANDA arrive in the background. They are escorted. They look frantic.

EDDIE looks at DS FRANK, okay to go forward? DS FRANK shakes her head.

EDDIE
We're here now, Jamie. We're here.

JAMIE turns and sees his dad as they are taken into another room, the family room. PC JENKINS, late twenties, emerges from it.

JAMIE
Can I go to them?

SGT GOLDING
The sooner we process you here, son, the sooner we can bring your dad in. You're doing really well, just concentrate for me, Jamie. Once you've had your breakfast, you're going to be visited by a healthcare professional and then if they think you're okay, we'll take you to have some photos and samples taken. And your lawyer will be brought in.

JAMIE
What kind of samples?

SGT GOLDING
That’s not a question I know the answer to just now. PC Jenkins –

PC JENKINS
Hello Jamie, will you follow me?

JAMIE nods.

PC JENKINS leads him down the corridor into the cells.

INT. CELLS. HEYWOOD STREET POLICE STATION

PC JENKINS opens one of the cells.

PC JENKINS
Here we are, then.

JAMIE looks at him and nods.

He walks into the cell.

He sits. PC JENKINS takes a long look at him as if trying to work something out.

PC JENKINS (CONT’D)
This is a dry cell, so if you need the toilet, you’ll have to ask, okay?

JAMIE
Okay.

We look with him as JAMIE takes in his four walls, his wipe-clean bed.

And then PC JENKINS closes the door and bolts it.

He walks back to the custody suite.

INT. CUSTODY SUITE. HEYWOOD STREET POLICE STATION

SGT GOLDING is making notes in his computer.
DI BASCOMBE walks through and into the family room.

INT. FAMILY ROOM. HEYWOOD STREET POLICE STATION

EDDIE and MANDA sit together. LISA sits further off.

DI BASCOMBE
Mr and Mrs Miller, how's it going?

EDDIE
Brilliant, yeah.

DI BASCOMBE
I understand this must be a hard time for you, but I've got a few questions I need to ask if that's okay. Jamie has asked for a solicitor, do you have a solicitor you would like to work with?

EDDIE
No. No.

EDDIE looks across at MANDA. His brain is ticking at double the rate it should.

MANDA takes his hand and then puts it down again. Her brain is swimming.

DI BASCOMBE
Then there is a duty solicitor who can come, would you like me to get that call made?

EDDIE
One of yours is it?

DI BASCOMBE

They don't work for us, it's their duty to protect your son's interests. They're a facility that we have here that is offered free of charge - if asked for.

EDDIE

Yeah, but normally free don't mean good, right?

DI BASCOMBE

You can meet them and if you are unhappy, you say so and we'll work something else out. But in my experience, these solicitors are very competent.

EDDIE looks at MANDA. Who nods.

EDDIE

Go on then. Yeah.

MANDA

Thank you.

EDDIE

Thank you. Yeah. Yeah.

DI BASCOMBE

You alright, Mrs Miller?

MANDA

No. How can you behave like that, and come in here and behave like this. How does that work, eh? Your men threw me on the floor. Threw my daughter on the floor.

LISA

I'm okay.

DI BASCOMBE
(assertive)
I hope they didn't do that. I hope they told you to get on the floor. For your safety and their safety. If they didn't, you're well within your rights to make a complaint. Would you like me to get someone to come in?

LISA
That is what they did, Mum.

MANDA
Okay.

DI BASCOMBE nods.

DI BASCOMBE
Second thing. And – we have someone suitable if you feel unable to do it, that's fine, but he has asked that you be his appropriate adult, Mr Miller –

EDDIE looks up. Both him and MANDA are surprised. LISA isn't as surprised.

EDDIE
He wants me?

MANDA
What? Why?

DI BASCOMBE
This means being with him when he meets his healthcare professional, for his searches, for his samples being taken and for the interview.

EDDIE
Yeah.

MANDA
Why did he pick you? He's not good with needles.

EDDIE
No.

DI BASCOMBE
Mr Miller, this is important, if your son has given you any admission as to any of the events for which he is being arrested then you can't do the job, it'd prejudice the case, and damage your son's legal prospects...

EDDIE looks at DI BASCOMBE with an open face.

EDDIE
He didn't say anything and he hasn't done anything.

Beat.

EDDIE (CONT'D)
Yes. I'm ready. I can do it.

DI BASCOMBE looks at him carefully.

DI BASCOMBE
Okay. The healthcare professional will be with you soon, she's running a bit late, you'll be taken through when she is. There is a coffee machine there, it's not great but it is drinkable, try to sit down and take a breath.

EDDIE
Yeah. Thank you.

DI BASCOMBE leaves.

EDDIE stands up as if to follow him and then sits back down.

EDDIE (CONT'D)
At least I'll see him.

He looks at his wife.

EDDIE (CONT'D)
Do you want a coffee, love?

MANDA
No thanks.

MANDA gets out her phone.

She begins to text someone. EDDIE looks at her, deeply unsure.

EDDIE
Love, I don't think it's a good idea to be telling people about this till we understand it, yeah?

MANDA
I'm texting Susie to make sure our house is okay.

EDDIE says nothing. His leg moves up and down.

MANDA (CONT'D)
We haven't got a door any more if you remember.

EDDIE nods. MANDA continues to text. He looks at his daughter.

EDDIE
Maybe you should be at home.

LISA
And what would I do there? Let me stay. Please.

EDDIE is unable to sit still.

EDDIE turns to MANDA, still deep in her phone. He thinks and then sits beside her.

EDDIE
Tell your sister to take pictures of everything. Don't clean anything up.

MANDA
Good idea.

LISA
Mum, what's going to happen?

MANDA
It's alright, love, it's just a mistake. You see it on the telly all the time, it's just a mistake.

EDDIE
She said they were charging him with murder.

LISA
Well he hasn't done anything has he!

EDDIE
Of course he hasn't.

DS FRANK walks past the door and EDDIE dashes out to her...

EDDIE (CONT'D)
Excuse me, you were at our house weren't you?

DS FRANK
Yeah.

EDDIE
Can you tell me when I can see my son?

DS FRANK
Not long, Mr Miller, alright?

She carries on through into the station.

We catch one last look at EDDIE as she walks through.

His miserable face is all-consuming.

INT. HEYWOOD STREET POLICE STATION

We keep pace with DS FRANK, who walks fast.

The station is alive with noise. Officers going about different sorts of duties. This is real, a hub of effort.

We may catch glimpses and snippets of other business.

We may not. We force our way through it alongside DS FRANK, as she heads into the –

INT. INCIDENT ROOM. HEYWOOD STREET POLICE STATION

DS FRANK
How much do you want a cigarette right now?

DI BASCOMBE smiles and throws a juggling ball between two hands. He has energy to burn.

DS FRANK (CONT'D)
Anything from upstairs?

DI BASCOMBE
Comms wanting to know what to release when – but nothing from the DCI.

Beat. He throws the ball again.

DI BASCOMBE (CONT'D)
Are you worried about the dad.

DS FRANK
The dad? No, I'm not worried about the dad - why, what you saying?

DI BASCOMBE
I don't know - I had this old case once, young boy. Put it this way, it wasn't till months later we found out what his dad was doing to him.

DS FRANK
I don't see it, I don't.

DI BASCOMBE
(considering)
No. I don't either.

DI BASCOMBE stands and walks about the room. We see the agitation inside him. He can't stay still.

DI BASCOMBE (CONT'D)
Any updates from forensics?

DS FRANK
You think they'll have an answer already?

DI BASCOMBE
They'll have been through a good chunk of the house by now - they got the shoes? Any possible weapon?

DS FRANK
I'll check in.

DI BASCOMBE
What about Bruntwood, have they sent over the files yet?

DS FRANK
I don't think anyone's actually been in the school. It's early yet. I'll give them a call. Rush it up.

DI BASCOMBE
Okay. Are we in his phone yet?

DS FRANK
It's locked.

DI BASCOMBE sits down again.

DI BASCOMBE
Can we ask for his code?

DS FRANK
Not till the assessment is done.

DI BASCOMBE
And she's late.

DS FRANK nods. DI BASCOMBE sways on his chair.

DI BASCOMBE (CONT'D)
Shall we go through the plan again?

DS FRANK
We could. But I honestly think we're good.

DI BASCOMBE nods.

He picks up an apple from his desk, he throws it from hand to hand.

He walks out. We travel with him. Past pictures on the wall that show JAMIE on CCTV.

We do not linger for a second on this.

INT. STAIRCASE. HEYWOOD STREET POLICE STATION

PC JENKINS slides in to walk beside him.

PC JENKINS
Sir, I'm just going through the PER form.

DI BASCOMBE
Yeah.

PC JENKINS
Post charge, sir. He's underage. The council will need to decide which accommodation he can be moved to.

They see ERICA hurrying past at the bottom of the stairs.

DI BASCOMBE
(calling down to her)
Nice of you to join us...

ERICA
(fuck you)
Do you know what time it is?

She keeps going on. DI BASCOMBE looks irritated and turns to PC JENKINS with condescension.

DI BASCOMBE
I don't know what you're asking me.

PC JENKINS
I'm asking for a risk assessment.

DI BASCOMBE
He's accused of murdering someone with a kitchen knife.

PC JENKINS
So where are they going to put him?

DI BASCOMBE
That’s a mountain for later, son. Yeah?

PC JENKINS nods, and scurries off. DI BASCOMBE looks on darkly.

INT. CORRIDOR. HEYWOOD STREET POLICE STATION

He stands still.

Just for a moment.

He takes a bite of the apple.

He controls his breath.

He takes out his phone and rings. Text in brackets is replies that we may only vaguely hear.

PHONE
(Hi.)

DI BASCOMBE
Good time, bad time?

PHONE
(Early time.)

DI BASCOMBE
Sorry, know it’s early...

PHONE
(I was in the shower.)

DI BASCOMBE
Did Adam go in?

PHONE
(To school? It’s not even half six...)

DI BASCOMBE
Sorry. But he’s going in?

PHONE
(He text you?)

DI BASCOMBE
Yeah, he texted, I ignored it

PHONE
(Good. Stay ignoring it.)

DI BASCOMBE
I told Misha I couldn't be trusted, soft touch I said.

PHONE
(I bet she agreed...)

DI BASCOMBE smiles.

DI BASCOMBE
Okay. Just wanted to say hi.

PHONE
(Hi, you okay?)

DI BASCOMBE
I'm fine. I'm fine. Better go.

PHONE
(I love you.)

DI BASCOMBE
You too - bye.

He disconnects. He takes another bite of the apple.

And then PC JENKINS comes down the stairs holding a form.

PC JENKINS
Sir.

DI BASCOMBE nods and then carries on down the corridor, into the life of the station.

And we walk with PC JENKINS.

INT. CUSTODY SUITE. HEYWOOD STREET POLICE STATION

The door swings open and a police officer comes through with a cut above his eye.

We pass that story and continue on into this story.

We travel past SGT GOLDING, who is on the phone.

We turn, with PC JENKINS, through towards the cells.

PC JENKINS knocks.

The door is opened, and PC JENKINS hands ERICA the form.

PC JENKINS
Sorry.

ERICA
That's okay, cheers.

INT. CELLS. HEYWOOD STREET POLICE STATION

ERICA sits back down as the door closes, and looks at JAMIE intently.

EDDIE is stood by the door. He's staring at his son.

We notice the cornflakes and a carton of juice on a tray on the floor.

They haven't been touched.

ERICA
Okay Jamie, just a few more questions if that's okay. Can you explain to me what being under arrest means?

JAMIE
It means being here.

ERICA smiles kindly.

ERICA
Can you have another go at that?

EDDIE
Answer the question, Jamie.

ERICA doesn't need EDDIE's help.

JAMIE
It means the police think I done something and they want me locked up till they know whether I have.

ERICA
That's a good answer. Can you explain why you might need a lawyer?

JAMIE
So I don't get trapped saying the wrong thing?

ERICA
Also a good answer. Okay. Jamie. I think you're a bright boy and I don't see a vulnerability here that the police need to be aware of. Do you have any questions for me?

JAMIE
Yeah. Is that a bad thing?

ERICA
You're doing fine. I'll give you two a minute.

EDDIE sits down with JAMIE on his bed.

EDDIE
You need to eat your cornflakes.

JAMIE
I don't want them.

EDDIE
Eat them, Jamie. You need to eat something.

He looks at his dad. His emotions get the better of him.

JAMIE
I didn't do anything. I just want to go home, I've not done anything.

EDDIE holds back.

EDDIE
Then this'll be over quick.

JAMIE
That means you think I did.

EDDIE
No. They just -

JAMIE
- You believe me? I didn't do anything.

EDDIE
Course I do, you're my Jamie.

ERICA knocks on the door. PC JENKINS is still waiting outside.

ERICA
Sorry Mr Miller - I'm going to have to ask you to leave if that's okay.

She walks out.

EDDIE follows ERICA out.

EDDIE
Eat your cornflakes.

He turns and watches as JAMIE takes a miserable bite.

EDDIE nods and follows PC JENKINS as they walk into the custody suite.

EDDIE (CONT'D)
How long's he going to be here, mate?

PC JENKINS
I can't answer that unfortunately.

EDDIE
You haven't got an idea?

EDDIE goes back into the family room. We stay with ERICA.

INT. CUSTODY SUITE. HEYWOOD STREET POLICE STATION

ERICA fills in the form. She does so rapidly. She knows her way around it.

ERICA
A bright boy. No current medication, no relevant medical history.

She looks at SGT GOLDING grimly.

ERICA (CONT'D)
I don't like juvenile cases.

SGT GOLDING
No one likes them.

ERICA nods and turns back to the form.

PAULIE BARLOW, mid-thirties, focused, enters with a smile.

PAULIE
Hello again, sergeant. Jamie Miller?

SGT GOLDING
His parents are in the family room. He's in a cell. Parents first?

PAULIE
Thank you.

SGT GOLDING picks up a phone, we follow PAULIE as he walks over to the family room towards –

INT. FAMILY ROOM. HEYWOOD STREET POLICE STATION

- EDDIE and MANDA. LISA is sitting further off on her phone.

PAULIE
Mr and Mrs Miller? My name is Paul Barlow. I'm from Storey and French.

He hands them his card.

PAULIE (CONT'D)
I have been allocated Jamie's case.

EDDIE
Finally. What do they know? What's going on?

PAULIE sits down beside them.

PAULIE
So the way this works is I will be briefed by the custody sergeant on what's been going on since Jamie's arrest, and the arresting officers as to the particulars of the case.

EDDIE
Okay.

PAULIE
Do you have any complaints as to your treatment so far?

MANDA
They tore the house apart.

EDDIE
They had guns. They had -

PAULIE
When a violent death has taken place that is sometimes the name of the game. The question will be whether it was proportionate. That we will look at later. How's Jamie?

EDDIE and MANDA both blink uncomprehendingly at PAULIE.

EDDIE
He wants me as his appropriate adult.

PAULIE
Good. It's generally better he has a parent in there. You'll be able to keep him calm while we work this out.

MANDA looks at EDDIE - can he?

EDDIE
He seems – he's a mess.

PAULIE
I would be.

He shakes their hands.

PAULIE (CONT'D)
Nothing I can say will make this situation better. I can see the shock that's happened here. It's understandable. But we'll do our best here, okay? I'm going to get myself briefed, you sit tight and someone will come and get you shortly.

He stands and leaves the family room.

INT. CUSTODY SUITE. HEYWOOD STREET POLICE STATION

He heads back past SGT GOLDING.

PAULIE
Is it the usual room?

SGT GOLDING
All the way down.

He carries on to a side room. We wait on the outside of it.

And then we see DI BASCOMBE and DS FRANK coming down the corridor towards it.

They enter the room and we follow them in.

INT. INTERVIEW ROOM. HEYWOOD STREET POLICE STATION

DI BASCOMBE
Hello Paul.

PAULIE
What have we got?

DI BASCOMBE slides a piece of paper across the table to PAULIE.

DI BASCOMBE
Incident took place at ten-thirteen p.m. last night. Arrest took place –

DI BASCOMBE checks his watch.

DI BASCOMBE (CONT'D)
I make it thirty-four minutes ago.

PAULIE
That's my personal record broken then. Apparently you screwed up the house.

DI BASCOMBE
Sorry about that.

PAULIE reads over the paper.

PAULIE
Murder, so I'm assuming you'll be going after possession and threatening as well then?

DI BASCOMBE
Yup.

PAULIE
Can I know anything about the victim?

DI BASCOMBE
You will do.

PAULIE
Media blackout is it? Because I couldn't see anything –

DI BASCOMBE
We're still trying to find their relatives – their dad.

PAULIE nods.

PAULIE
Has he been told his right to silence?

DI BASCOMBE
Yes.

PAULIE
Is he clear on what that means?

DI BASCOMBE
Yes.

PAULIE
Has he been fed?

DI BASCOMBE
He's been given the opportunity to eat.

PAULIE
Assessed?

DS FRANK
She passed him fit.

PAULIE
Searched?

DI BASCOMBE
We waited for you.

PAULIE keeps scanning the document.

PAULIE
You're taking blood?

DI BASCOMBE
There's scratches on his arms and blood at the scene. It's not without justification.

PAULIE
I wasn't questioning that.

PAULIE reads some more. They watch.

He churns over the words.

PAULIE (CONT'D)
What investigation otherwise has taken place so far?

DI BASCOMBE
Nothing with the suspect.

PAULIE
Anything else I need to know?

DI BASCOMBE
Nothing else that we'll tell you now.

PAULIE nods. He knows the drill.

PAULIE
When was the victim pronounced?

DI BASCOMBE
At the scene. There were multiple wounds as it says there.

PAULIE digests this.

PAULIE
The father's his appropriate adult?

DI BASCOMBE
Yes.

PAULIE
He okay?

DI BASCOMBE
We think so.

PAULIE
How's Jamie around him?

DI BASCOMBE
We don't know.

SGT GOLDING puts his head in.

SGT GOLDING
We're ready for samples when you are.

PAULIE
That's all I'm getting?

DI BASCOMBE
That's all we can help with right now.

PAULIE
Okay. Samples then a chat. Give me a chance to look at him first.

He holds out a hand, he shakes them both in turn.

DI BASCOMBE
Don't be excited, Paul.

PAULIE
I'm not excited.

DI BASCOMBE
Makes you look a bit of a prick.

PAULIE takes that - they know each other well - he nods.

They exit.

We follow SGT GOLDING.

We watch PAULIE's face as SGT GOLDING walks away from him.

PAULIE
DI Bascombe? One last thing?

DI BASCOMBE lets him pursue him. A PC falls in beside them.

PC WILKINS
Sir, we have a teacher here from Bruntwood Academy?

DI BASCOMBE
You have two minutes, and then I need to go...

We stay with SGT GOLDING.

INT. FAMILY ROOM. HEYWOOD STREET POLICE STATION

SGT GOLDING walks into the family room.

SGT GOLDING
Can I have Mr Miller please?

EDDIE stands, shooting a look to MANDA.

SGT GOLDING (CONT'D)
We just need you in the medical suite for your son to have his samples taken.

MANDA
Watch him with the needles.

EDDIE follows SGT GOLDING through to the medical suite.

INT. MEDICAL CUBICLE. HEYWOOD STREET POLICE STATION

ERICA is waiting.

SGT GOLDING
We'll fetch Jamie and be back with you shortly.

ERICA and EDDIE wait.

Eventually, PC JENKINS brings JAMIE in. PG GROGAN follows them.

PC JENKINS
Jamie, this is PC Grogan. I'm going take your photo and then I'm going to search you, and then Erica's going to take some samples, okay?

JAMIE
Okay.

PC JENKINS
Let's put you against this wall for the photo can we?

JAMIE
Okay.

PC JENKINS
There'll be a bit of a flash.

He stands against the wall. Photos are taken.

PC JENKINS (CONT'D)
And to the side.

PAULIE enters at the back of the room. He reads the paper he's been given again.

He nods at EDDIE, who nods back.

PC JENKINS (CONT'D)
And the other side.

PAULIE
Jamie, my name is Paul Barlow, I'm from a solicitor firm called

Storey and French and I will be advising you today, okay?

JAMIE

Okay.

PAULIE

We'll talk in a bit, but I didn't want you wondering who this strange man was, okay?

ERICA

Now I'm going to need to take a cheek swab, okay? So open wide.

JAMIE opens wide. ERICA takes a cheek swab. As she does, PC GROGAN gets ready the fingerprint scanner.

PC JENKINS

Okay, and let's take fingerprints. Put your right thumb down on there.

We close on EDDIE's face.

We just study it as he watches his son.

PC JENKINS (CONT'D)

Your index finger. Thank you. Your middle finger. Thank you. Your ring finger. Thank you. Your little finger. Thank you.

PC JENKINS nods. But we turn back to EDDIE.

We watch his gently searching face.

He looks to the side and sees that PAULIE is looking at his phone.

PC JENKINS (CONT'D)

Now the other side. Your left thumb. Thank you. Your index finger. Press it down really hard. Thank you. Your middle finger. Thank you. Your ring finger. Thank you. Your little finger. Thank you.

PC GROGAN has got a tray ready.

PC JENKINS (CONT'D)
Jamie. We need your passcode please? So we can access your phone.

PAULIE
There's no need to tell them that.

JAMIE
Okay.

PC JENKINS
Can we have your passcode?

JAMIE
No.

PC JENKINS
Okay, now Erica's going to take a blood specimen.

JAMIE
I don't like needles.

EDDIE
He's no good with them.

PC JENKINS
I'm afraid it may harm your defence if you refuse.

JAMIE looks at PAULIE.

PAULIE
He's right.

PC JENKINS turns to face EDDIE.

PC JENKINS
Do you consent to your son providing a specimen?

EDDIE
Fine. Just look at me, Jamie.

JAMIE
Okay.

ERICA preps JAMIE's arm.

EDDIE
Look me in the eyes.

The two hold eye contact as ERICA takes a syringe of blood. It hurts JAMIE.

ERICA
It's done.

EDDIE
Good boy.

JAMIE winces, his dad smiles. ERICA exits with the sample.

PC JENKINS
Okay. And now I'm going to ask you to take your clothes off.

JAMIE
All of them?

PC JENKINS
I need to undertake a strip search.

PAULIE
Is that necessary?

PC JENKINS
I'm afraid so.

JAMIE looks at his dad, who isn't sure what to say.

EDDIE
I'm not too sure about this.

PC JENKINS
There is a chance he has concealed things on or around his body.

EDDIE
He wet himself so he already changed his trousers.

PC JENKINS
This is a serious offence. I've scratch marks already marked in the file on his left arm.

EDDIE looks at the scratch marks, he hadn't seen them.

PC JENKINS (CONT'D)
I need to be able to see if there are other marks we might need to know about, bruising, cuts, et cetera.

EDDIE
It's just - that's a serious thing to do to a thirteen-year-old boy. You want your bits looked at when you were thirteen did you?

PC JENKINS
I wasn't accused of a crime.

EDDIE
Accused. Not found guilty. Accused. Come on now. What can we do?

He turns to PAULIE.

PAULIE
I'm sorry, they're entitled to under PACE.

PC JENKINS
I promise I will be very careful.

EDDIE
I don't know you from Adam, kid.

PAULIE
Mr Miller, we need to cooperate - trust me - passcodes we can tell them no on, this -

JAMIE
I don't mind, Dad.

EDDIE looks up, shocked.

He takes a moment.

EDDIE nods.

PC JENKINS
I need to observe, and PC Grogan needs to observe me.

JAMIE
Okay.

PC JENKINS
If you take your clothes off, and put them on the side there -

ERICA and PAULIE turn around. We hold on EDDIE's face.

PC JENKINS (CONT'D)
Can you turn to face me? Arms up. And turn to the side. And turn around, face the wall behind you. You can put your arms down, and face forward to me again. Okay. Can you just lift up your

penis - we just need to see if there's defensive wounds on your scrotum -

EDDIE's entire body is ready to swing.

PC JENKINS (CONT'D)
And that's done. If I can ask you to put on these clothes, and we'll bag yours?

EDDIE
What you going to do with them?

PC JENKINS
Evidence.

JAMIE puts on the new clothes. A basic tracksuit. It's two sizes too big for him.

JAMIE
Okay Dad.

EDDIE's straight to JAMIE's side.

EDDIE
You okay? You alright?

JAMIE
Yeah.

EDDIE
You sure?

JAMIE
Yeah.

PAULIE
Can you give me a room to talk to my client?

PC JENKINS
One's been arranged next door. Follow me.

INT. CORRIDOR. HEYWOOD STREET POLICE STATION

They follow PC JENKINS, who opens the interview room next door. JAMIE, PAULIE and EDDIE file in.

INT. SOLICITORS' ROOM. HEYWOOD STREET POLICE STATION

PAULIE is nervous, we hadn't quite seen it before now.

EDDIE watches him carefully.

PAULIE
If you pop yourself there, Jamie, and Dad can sit next to you. I'm happy to say that's that done, okay? I thought you handled it extremely well.

JAMIE looks at him as they sit.

PAULIE (CONT'D)
What's your favourite subject in school?

JAMIE
Why does that matter?

PAULIE
Just – humour me –

JAMIE
History.

PAULIE
Why?

JAMIE
I – like the stories.

PAULIE
What's your favourite bit of history?

JAMIE
We're doing the Industrial Revolution.

PAULIE
Who do you like who took part in the Industrial Revolution?

JAMIE
You know Brunel?

PAULIE
I do.

JAMIE
I like him.

PAULIE
Why?

JAMIE
Because he did stuff no one else did. Boats. Trains. Everything. He just did it.

PAULIE looks at him and smiles. He looks at EDDIE.

PAULIE
Clever kid.

EDDIE says nothing, still working PAULIE out.

PAULIE (CONT'D)
I'm not asking you whether or not you did it, Jamie.

JAMIE
I didn't.

EDDIE
He didn't, no way.

PAULIE
My job - and your dad's job - is to protect you *whatever* happened last night.

JAMIE nods.

PAULIE (CONT'D)
The police are trying to understand what happened. But they're not trying to protect you, they believe you're guilty of something, that's why we're here.

JAMIE
I didn't do anything.

PAULIE
So you say 'no comment', okay? Just 'no comment'.

JAMIE
To everything?

PAULIE
Not to everything, no. That won't go down well. Just to any questions about the events of last night. Will you be able to tell the difference? Between questions you should answer and questions you should not?

JAMIE
I don't know -

PAULIE
Is your name Jamie?

JAMIE
Yes.

PAULIE
Where were you last night, Jamie?

JAMIE
No comment.

PAULIE gives him a thumbs-up. JAMIE nods.

PAULIE

That's it. Any time you're not sure, anytime it's fifty-fifty - 'no comment' and if I think you should answer, I'll advise so. You're a bright lad. You'll do fine. I will be there. Your dad will be there. I won't be afraid to speak up, your dad can also speak up whenever he chooses.

EDDIE

Can I?

PAULIE

Of course you can.

Beat.

JAMIE

I didn't do anything wrong.

PAULIE

Then that makes it easy. Right, give me a minute, I'll just see how they're getting on setting up, sit tight for me. I'll be back.

PAULIE exits the room. EDDIE thinks and then exits past two police officers and travels with him.

EDDIE

Give me a second, Jamie.

JAMIE is left.

INT. CORRIDOR. HEYWOOD STREET POLICE STATION

PAULIE is walking quickly away, he notices EDDIE catch up with him.

PAULIE
How are we doing here?

EDDIE
I haven't got a clue what I'm doing. I just say anything? Anything I want?

PAULIE
Don't overuse it. And don't answer for him. Just be yourself, they know you're his dad, we know you're his dad, it's okay to be shocked, it's okay to process, it's okay to be human.

EDDIE
Because I'm just - this isn't normal, you know? And I was working last night, I haven't - slept. I've never even been in a police station before.

PAULIE
You'll be fine.

EDDIE
I don't want to get it wrong.

PAULIE
You'll be fine.

EDDIE cracks.

EDDIE
(adamant)
I'm shitting it. I'm a good dad, he's a good kid. He's not the kind of kid who'd do this.

PAULIE turns, no-nonsense.

PAULIE
And now this has happened, and here we are. And I think the

police have pretty compelling evidence otherwise they wouldn't have been able to ask for blood or make the entrance they did. I don't know what that evidence is, but I think it'll be clear to us very soon. So raise that chin up, be the 'good dad', and suck it up, okay?

EDDIE looks at him a moment more, and then nods.

PAULIE (CONT'D)
Great. Thank you.

The camera picks out DI BASCOMBE and DS FRANK entering a room ahead of them.

PAULIE (CONT'D)
They're shaping up for the interview. I need a minute to look everything through. Can you go sit with him?

EDDIE nods again. He pulls himself together.

He returns to the room with his son inside.

INT. SOLICITORS' ROOM. HEYWOOD STREET POLICE STATION

JAMIE is sat in silence.

EDDIE sits beside him in silence.

The door gently closes.

He opens his mouth to say something, but he doesn't know what to say.

So they just sit there. Both absolutely fucked.

And we watch them sit.

There is still love in this room.

But it feels remote.

And impossible to access.

EDDIE rouses himself. He forces himself upright.

It's an almost heroic act.

EDDIE
I'm here, okay? I'm here.

JAMIE
Yeah.

EDDIE
You understand me, Jamie? I'm here.

JAMIE
Yeah.

EDDIE
Look at me.

JAMIE looks up at his dad.

EDDIE (CONT'D)
I'm going to ask you once, okay? No matter what's happened, what you have or haven't done - I want you to tell me the truth. Okay?

JAMIE holds EDDIE's eye.

EDDIE (CONT'D)
Did you do it?

JAMIE shakes his head.

JAMIE
No.

EDDIE
Promise?

JAMIE

I promise.

EDDIE

Good. Okay.

EDDIE nearly breaks again.

EDDIE (CONT'D)

Okay then, everything's going to be alright then, isn't it?

PAULIE re-enters.

PAULIE

Okay. They're ready.

EDDIE

Okay, yeah so are we.

JAMIE stands up mechanically, EDDIE looks at his young back softly.

JAMIE follows PAULIE.

EDDIE takes a moment and then follows them both.

INT. CORRIDOR. HEYWOOD STREET POLICE STATION

They walk quickly down the corridor -

PAULIE

Just before we go in, Jamie, to go over what we said again, if you're not sure just look at me, and remember that 'no comment'. Your dad will be with you all the way through.

- and enter a new room -

INT. INTERVIEW ROOM. HEYWOOD STREET POLICE STATION

Where DI BASCOMBE and DS FRANK are waiting for them.

DI BASCOMBE

Let's have you here - here - and here. Thank you.

They sit.

DI BASCOMBE (CONT'D)

Over there you'll see this interview is being recorded. We have audio and video. Okay Jamie?

JAMIE

Yes.

DI BASCOMBE

Great, starting recording now, then.

DS FRANK stands and sets the camcorder going, whilst DI BASCOMBE begins the digital audio recording device - they all wait for the long, loud beep to stop before going on.

DI BASCOMBE (CONT'D)

I'm going to remind you of your rights now. I want you to really listen to this. You do not have to say anything. But, it may harm your defence if you do not mention, when questioned, something which you later rely on in court. Anything you do say may be given in evidence. Okay?

JAMIE

Yes.

DI BASCOMBE nods.

DI BASCOMBE
I am DI Bascombe, also in attendance is DS Frank. We are talking to Jamie Miller, and his appropriate adult Eddie Miller, and his lawyer Paul Barlow. It is six-fifty-eight a.m.

Beat.

DI BASCOMBE (CONT'D)
Hello Jamie.

JAMIE
Hello.

DI BASCOMBE
I want to first of all ask you what you did last night?

JAMIE
Last night?

PAULIE
Jamie -

DI BASCOMBE
Not so long ago to forget.

JAMIE looks at PAULIE.

JAMIE
No comment.

DI BASCOMBE
What did you do?

JAMIE
No comment.

DI BASCOMBE
That's not helpful, Jamie.

JAMIE
Sorry.

DI BASCOMBE nods.

DI BASCOMBE
Okay. Let's move on to something you can talk about. I've been reading your school reports.

JAMIE
Why?

DI BASCOMBE
I got the school to send them over.

JAMIE
Yeah.

DI BASCOMBE
The teachers expect big things, reading between the lines. You're a good student. Do you want to do A levels do you think?

JAMIE looks at EDDIE.

PAULIE
You can answer, Jamie.

JAMIE
I don't know.

DI BASCOMBE
They do talk about some problems you've been having with your behaviour in recent months. The last year or so.

JAMIE
Yeah.

DI BASCOMBE
Why is that? What's been the problem?

JAMIE
I – don't know.

DI BASCOMBE
Have you got good friends?

JAMIE
Yeah.

DI BASCOMBE
Who are your good friends?

JAMIE
No comment.

DI BASCOMBE
You won't get them in any trouble.

JAMIE
But you – battered my door down this morning. So not sure you can say that.

DI BASCOMBE looks at DS FRANK – they note the clever answer.

DI BASCOMBE
That's fair.

Beat.

DI BASCOMBE (CONT'D)
I need to ask you about romantic relationships. Sexual relationships.

JAMIE
Why?

DI BASCOMBE
On your Instagram I noticed you reposted some pictures of a model...

He passes across some pictures of a woman in lingerie.

DI BASCOMBE (CONT'D)
What's her name?

JAMIE
I just like her pictures.

DI BASCOMBE
You don't know?

JAMIE
No.

DI BASCOMBE
You also - on your Instagram have pictures of this woman -

He passes across some pictures of another woman in lingerie.

DI BASCOMBE (CONT'D)
And this woman.

He passes across another set.

DI BASCOMBE (CONT'D)
Below this picture, which is the most recent one, there's a series of comments and innuendos - some quite aggressive. From you. How do you feel about women, Jamie?

JAMIE's face is burning. EDDIE looks at his son warily. What is this now?

EDDIE
What kind of a question is that?

DI BASCOMBE
Are you attracted to women?

JAMIE
Yeah.

DI BASCOMBE
Are these your type? Of women? Are these the sort of women you're attracted to?

JAMIE
Yeah.

DI BASCOMBE
Have you got a girlfriend?

JAMIE
No.

DI BASCOMBE
But if you did - you'd want a girlfriend to look like this?

JAMIE
No. They're too old.

Beat. DI BASCOMBE smiles.

DI BASCOMBE
Of course they are.

Beat.

DI BASCOMBE (CONT'D)
You also put up pictures of you and what I think are - friends?

He brings out some other pictures.

DI BASCOMBE (CONT'D)
Where was this picture taken?

JAMIE
I don't know. Train station maybe.

DI BASCOMBE
Who are these boys?

Beat.

DI BASCOMBE (CONT'D)
I understand you don't want to get them into trouble - but they're not in trouble, I'm just trying to build a picture.

DS FRANK
It won't be hard for us to find them. You're a clever kid, you can see that.

JAMIE looks to EDDIE.

EDDIE
Go ahead.

JAMIE
That's Tommy. That's Ryan.

DI BASCOMBE
Good friends?

JAMIE
Yeah.

DI BASCOMBE looks at EDDIE, almost checking whether he knows them too. EDDIE says nothing.

DI BASCOMBE
They recur in a lot of photos.

JAMIE
Only because Tommy tags me in stuff.

DI BASCOMBE
Is it always you three - out together?

JAMIE
I guess so.

DI BASCOMBE
You've known them a long time?

JAMIE looks at PAULIE, who nods.

JAMIE
Year One Tommy - Ryan came in Year Four.

DI BASCOMBE
What's - fun - for you guys? What do you like to do?

JAMIE
I don't know.

DI BASCOMBE
Sport? Films? Music?

JAMIE
Just going into town.

DI BASCOMBE
Hanging out?

JAMIE
Yeah.

Beat.

DI BASCOMBE
Were you with them last night?

JAMIE looks at PAULIE, who nods.

JAMIE
No comment.

DI BASCOMBE
What time did you get home?

JAMIE
No comment.

DI BASCOMBE
Okay. Okay. I understand. Everyone's doing their job here. That's fine. I recommended you get a lawyer, didn't I, Jamie?

JAMIE
Yeah.

He looks at PAULIE.

DI BASCOMBE
May I ask what you were wearing last night?

JAMIE
I don't remember.

DI BASCOMBE
Okay. Our scene-of-the-crime officers – the ones you saw in your house earlier – haven't found the clothes you wore last night but do think they've found the trainers.

He produces a photo.

DI BASCOMBE (CONT'D)
Can you identify these as your trainers?

JAMIE
I'm not sure. It's hard in a photo.

DI BASCOMBE
Do you own a pair of Nike Air Max shoes in a blue?

JAMIE
Yes.

DI BASCOMBE
Thank you.

Beat.

DI BASCOMBE (CONT'D)
And were you wearing them last night?

JAMIE
Maybe. Probably. I don't know.

DI BASCOMBE sits back, he nods at DS FRANK.

DS FRANK
Jamie, do you know a girl called Katie Leonard?

JAMIE looks at DS FRANK.

JAMIE
Yes.

She slides a picture of Katie Leonard across to JAMIE, DI BASCOMBE watches carefully as JAMIE looks at her and then nods.

DS FRANK
She's not in your reg group, but you share some classes, that's right isn't it?

JAMIE
English.

DS FRANK
Top set English. And maths and French. Set two. Very good.

Beat.

DS FRANK (CONT'D)
Do you two get on?

JAMIE
Yeah.

DS FRANK
You'd describe each other as friends?

JAMIE
I don't know.

DS FRANK
She occasionally comments on your Instagram posts. That's probably a sign you were friends, right?

JAMIE
I don't know. Maybe.

DS FRANK
Do you think other people would describe you two as friends?

JAMIE thinks, there's a long silence.

JAMIE
Is she who's dead?

There's a silence. DS FRANK looks at DI BASCOMBE.

DI BASCOMBE
Why would you ask that?

JAMIE
Is she?

DI BASCOMBE
Yes. She is. And we believe you know that. Clever - to ask the question - if that is the case.

PAULIE
Careful, DI Bascombe.

DI BASCOMBE flashes PAULIE a warning look.

EDDIE looks at JAMIE, who is sitting back, his eyes flickering slightly.

DS FRANK
How would you describe your friendship?

JAMIE
No comment.

DS FRANK
You seemed prepared to talk about your other friendships - but not this one - can you say why?

PAULIE
I think it's pretty clear why, wouldn't you say?

DS FRANK
Jamie?

JAMIE
We knew each other at school but not out of school.

DS FRANK
Was it a relationship that ever went beyond friendship?

JAMIE
I wouldn't even describe it as a friendship, so...

DS FRANK
Were you attracted to her?

JAMIE
No.

DS FRANK
Was there anything that could be described as sexual between you two?

EDDIE
He's thirteen years old.

DS FRANK
I know. Could you answer the question, Jamie?

JAMIE
No.

He takes a beat.

DI BASCOMBE
Was she who you were going to see last night, Jamie? Were you going to see her?

JAMIE
No.

DS FRANK
Her parents have told us she left the house at eight-thirty - was she coming to see you?

JAMIE
I told you, we weren't even mates.

DI BASCOMBE
But you did see her, didn't you?

JAMIE
No.

DI BASCOMBE
Her body was found in Crowthers car park. At just past ten-thirty p.m. Paramedics attended the scene. But weren't able to stop the bleeding. It was confirmed as being less than an hour since she'd been killed. So that means between nine-thirty and ten-thirty. What were you doing at that time?

JAMIE
I don't know.

DI BASCOMBE
But you were out?

PAULIE makes a subtle sign, JAMIE reads it.

JAMIE
No comment.

DI BASCOMBE
If I were to ask your dad here what time you were home?

EDDIE
I was on a late job. I'd only just got in when you came.

PAULIE
And you're not interviewing Mr Miller.

DI BASCOMBE
No.

DS FRANK
Were you meeting her there, or did you follow her there?

JAMIE
No. Neither.

DI BASCOMBE
Did you kill her, Jamie?

JAMIE
No.

DI BASCOMBE
You didn't kill her?

JAMIE
No. I didn't. You got me confused or something with someone else.

DI BASCOMBE
Okay.

DS FRANK
Do you know how many times she was stabbed, Jamie?

JAMIE

No.

DI BASCOMBE

She was stabbed seven times with a kitchen knife. She was stabbed all over, from her neck, to her arm, to her thigh, to her chest.

A tear rolls down JAMIE's face.

DI BASCOMBE (CONT'D)

That's a lot of stabbing.

DS FRANK

Does that upset you, Jamie?

EDDIE

Course it does.

DI BASCOMBE reaches into his bag. He pulls out a laptop.

DI BASCOMBE

You know what CCTV is, don't you?

JAMIE is now crying. EDDIE's eyes darken.

PAULIE

Perhaps now is a good point for us to take a break?

EDDIE sees JAMIE shake his head.

PAULIE (CONT'D)

Have a private consultation?

EDDIE

Is that what you want, Jamie?

JAMIE looks at his dad, conflicted.

JAMIE

No, I want to - carry on.

PAULIE
I really would insist on it -

EDDIE
I don't think it's a good idea. He wants to carry on, 'cause he's told them - he's not even her friend, he doesn't really know her even. He's got nothing to hide, so he's going to tell you.

DI BASCOMBE
Good. We've been looking through for images of you and Katie last night. Looking through council footage and contacting local businesses, even at this hour, for copies of any security tapes they have.

DS FRANK
We've managed to put together a timeline for your movements and hers.

They show him a picture.

DI BASCOMBE
This is you isn't it?

JAMIE just looks at the picture, it's clearly him. He continues to sob.

DI BASCOMBE
From this we were able to observe exactly what you were wearing. From your jeans, to your top, to your blue Nike Air Max.

JAMIE says nothing. EDDIE looks across at his son.

DI BASCOMBE (CONT'D)
This is you in Meadows Square at seven-forty-three, where you stayed for an hour. You're

talking to your friends - we believe that is Tommy, we're not sure if that is Ryan. And then you left them.

DS FRANK

And you walked around for a long time.

DI BASCOMBE

This is you outside the Battered Plaice at nine-oh-two p.m. This is you outside the library at nine-seventeen p.m. This is you outside JCR at nine-twenty-three p.m.

JAMIE

Yeah.

DI BASCOMBE

And then we see pictures of Katie, and we don't see when you spotted her, but we do see you following her. You did follow her, didn't you, Jamie?

JAMIE looks at EDDIE, who has horror on his face.

JAMIE

Dad.

He's looking for approbation. He's looking for something.

EDDIE turns, surprised to be called on.

EDDIE

You answer the question, Jamie.

JAMIE looks at PAULIE, who knows this is screwed too.

The tears are falling freely from JAMIE's face now.

JAMIE
But I didn't –

DI BASCOMBE
This is Katie outside of the crossing on Granby Street at nine-forty-six. This is you outside the crossing at nine-forty-seven. We have repeated tape of the same taking place again and again. Why were you following her, Jamie?

JAMIE
I wasn't.

DI BASCOMBE
Did she know you were following her?

JAMIE
I wasn't.

DI BASCOMBE
Was there a problem between you?

JAMIE
No.

DI BASCOMBE
Jamie, you do need to explain what's happened here, if not now then some time soon, okay?

JAMIE
I didn't do anything wrong.

There's a silence.

They all know exactly what he's done.

DI BASCOMBE
We're going to play you some footage now of what happened in the car park when a confrontation

happened between you and Katie. There's no sound. The picture is grainy. But we can map both your movements here, and it's pretty clear it's the two of you.

He plays the tape.

It's of JAMIE confronting KATIE.

It's colour tape. But the quality is occasionally glitchy.

We see them argue, see them fiercely say things to one another.

Horrible, brutal things.

KATIE pushes JAMIE so hard he lands on the floor.

And then he's fast after her.

We watch the faces as they see the worst of it.

EDDIE, PAULIE, DI BASCOMBE, DS FRANK and JAMIE. EDDIE and JAMIE obviously most of all.

We see JAMIE repeatedly stab KATIE and it's like someone is stabbing EDDIE.

And then the tape ends.

We sit in the silence and horror.

For as long as it takes.

We look at EDDIE as he attempts to digest what he's seen. As he tries to work out what this room is.

DI BASCOMBE (CONT'D)
How did you get home without anyone seeing you?

JAMIE
That isn't me.

DI BASCOMBE
You threw away your clothes. We don't have that on tape and we can't find the clothes – yet. But we think that happened. Your Nike Air Maxes you didn't throw away. Too expensive, am I right?

JAMIE bites his lip.

DI BASCOMBE (CONT'D)
We'll find her blood on those shoes, Jamie. And with this tape as evidence...

JAMIE says nothing. He's a mess.

DI BASCOMBE (CONT'D)
Do you want to say anything else, Jamie?

JAMIE
No.

DI BASCOMBE
Do you want to say what you've done here – do you want to explain it?

We focus increasingly on EDDIE, as we take the others in.

JAMIE
No – comment.

DI BASCOMBE
Do you want to give any reason as to why you could have done this?

JAMIE
I didn't.

DI BASCOMBE
Do you want to say sorry to her mum, who I had to talk to – at

past midnight last night - as she lay on the floor sobbing?

JAMIE

It wasn't me.

Those lying words echo in the faces of everyone present.

Even DI BASCOMBE has to compose himself a little.

DI BASCOMBE

Okay. Interview terminated at seven-twelve a.m. Okay.

He turns off the camcorder and the digital audio recording device, he nods to DS FRANK, and he and DS FRANK leave the room.

And we're left with JAMIE, EDDIE and PAULIE. The dregs of what is left in them slowly seeping away.

PAULIE

I'll give you two a minute.

PAULIE leaves.

JAMIE sobs the last of his tears out. He looks up. He looks at his dad. And we do too.

JAMIE

Dad?

EDDIE can't look at him.

JAMIE (CONT'D)

Dad?

There's a horrible pause. EDDIE really can't look at him.

JAMIE (CONT'D)

Dad? Dad?

JAMIE reaches for his dad. EDDIE flinches away.

EDDIE

What have you done? What have you done? Why?

He grabs for his son, holding him tight. They sob.

CREDITS.

EPISODE TWO

Ashley Walters (as DI Luke Bascombe), courtesy of Netflix © 2024

EXT. CAR PARK. SCHOOL

We are hard in on a shrine. There are flowers and teddy bears everywhere.

We see the words 'Katie' emblazoned everywhere.

And a sign:

'The Bruntwood Academy.
Excellence. Achievement. Friendship.
Come inside, and see the future.
Headmaster: William Hutchinson.'

The frame is broken by two police officers – DI BASCOMBE and DS FRANK are on their way in.

DS FRANK
We could have sent someone more junior.

INT. ENTRANCE HALL. SCHOOL

A nice woman is waiting for them.

DI BASCOMBE
Mrs Fenumore? I'm DI Bascombe. Thanks so much for doing this.

DS FRANK
DS Frank.

MRS FENUMORE
We've only just let them back. Everything might be a bit raw.

DI BASCOMBE
I know. We wouldn't be here if it wasn't important.

RYAN exits from the hall.

EXT. QUAD. SCHOOL

He sees TOMMY, he approaches him. He speaks in a low voice.

RYAN
The police are here.

TOMMY
Course they are. They're everywhere.

RYAN
I don't like it.

TOMMY
You're not in trouble.

RYAN isn't sure that's true. He takes a moment to think about it as he looks nervously about. Every kid is dangerous here.

RYAN
You heard from him?

TOMMY shakes his head.

RYAN (CONT'D)
Everyone's talking about him. I texted him.

TOMMY
I texted him.

RYAN checks his phone.

RYAN
I didn't hear anything. Did you?

TOMMY
Course not. He won't have his phone.

RYAN
You think it's true?

TOMMY
Course it is.

RYAN
You think he did it?

TOMMY
Yeah.

RYAN
They come to your house?

TOMMY
Yeah.

RYAN
They ask you how he got the knife?

TOMMY
Yeah.

RYAN
What did you say?

TOMMY
Dad said not to talk to you about it.

RYAN
Was he mad?

TOMMY
Fuck yeah. Weren't yours?

RYAN
No. They were - they just didn't say anything.

TOMMY nods, he knows what RYAN's guardians are like.

RYAN (CONT'D)
I don't want to be in trouble.

TOMMY
You're not in trouble.

RYAN
I don't want Jamie to be in trouble.

TOMMY
Yeah. Well. He is.

They walk into the canteen.

INT. CANTEEN. SCHOOL

It's full with the last of lunch.

We focus on one kid, ADAM, fifteen, shy, sad, lost in the middle of a crowd. He's alone.

He is looking across at a group of girls who are crying in an almost ritualistic manner. They are all Katie's age. They are all Katie's friends.

One of the girls looks up and sees ADAM. He immediately lowers his head.

He stays still for a moment, unsure what to do. He wants to look back to see whether she's still looking at him, but he won't.

His phone beeps. He looks at the text he's just got...it's a voice note...He cradles it close to his ear. We only hear part of it.

DI BASCOMBE (V.O.)
We had to come. Might have to go to your class. It'll be okay. I'll leave you alone I promise.

ADAM thinks, he picks up his tray and starts to walk. He passes others crying, people on phones, and pieces of conversation.

As he does, people put bits of their rubbish on his tray. They do so without looking at him. This is clearly an established ritual. ADAM notices it but does nothing.

ADAM keeps walking. He walks past the exuberant FREDO, who has spotted ADAM.

FREDO
Adam, give me one-twenty now for some pizza.

MR GARFIELD
Fredo, leave him alone now, you're on free lunches.

FREDO picks up someone else's rubbish to put on ADAM's tray.

ADAM just keeps walking. He hates FREDO and FREDO hates him.

The camera turns and makes after ADAM, who is walking fast away into the toilets.

INT. CORRIDOR. SCHOOL

We travel away from him, with two teachers, utterly consumed.

They speak with soft voices, they don't want to be overheard.

MR HUTCHINSON
I've had fourteen parents, fourteen - is your school safe?

MRS BAILEY
What do you say?

MR HUTCHINSON
I say the matter didn't happen on school property - and then they talk about security guards and metal detectors -

We pass a drum lesson - with a kid and a teacher going full pelt.

We stop at the open door and watch the kid really bash the drums.

MR HOLDSWORTH
Try and find the downbeat...Okay? Bah - BAH - bah - BAH.

We continue on - catching up with the teachers.

MRS BAILEY
Mia Taylor told me we need to open a grief support room.

MR HUTCHINSON
We're security guards and social workers, great.

MRS BAILEY
I'm worried about the impact it's gonna have on the kids. It's a lot.

MR HUTCHINSON
We'll keep an eye on it.

The school bell goes. Some kids walk down the stairs -

TAU
I say we go and fuck him up.

SHAUN
Nah, I heard he's in jail.

TAU
Yeah? We break in - and -

We pass DI BASCOMBE and DS FRANK, who are being led by MRS FENUMORE. She leads them into the building.

MRS FENUMORE approaches a student, a girl with smudged mascara. She has power.

MRS FENUMORE
Jade, could you pop inside the office for us? Please?

JADE stands, and MRS FENUMORE and DS FRANK follow her.

INT. PRIVATE ROOM. SCHOOL

DI BASCOMBE enters behind them.

DI BASCOMBE
Thanks for this, Jade. I'm DI Bascombe, this is DS Frank. And Mrs Fenumore has agreed to be here in order to keep an eye on things from the school's perspective. And offer you any support you might want or need. If that's okay.

JADE
I don't know you.

MRS FENUMORE
I teach in the lower school.

JADE looks at her distrustfully.

DI BASCOMBE
Jade, I'm - we're - grateful for this, thanks for agreeing to talk to us.

JADE
(so dry)
I agreed, did I? And I thought I just got pulled off break.

DI BASCOMBE
We tried to reach you at home, but your mum wasn't sure when you'd be back, this - if you don't mind...

JADE
I don't mind.

DI BASCOMBE ploughs on.

DI BASCOMBE
I'm the investigating officer in Katie's case, okay? I'm from Heywood Street Station, and there's a crime reference number on the back of my card here -

DI BASCOMBE writes on the back of a business card.

DI BASCOMBE (CONT'D)
Use that reference any time you want to know the progress on the case.

JADE
That's a bit flash, don't you think?

He puts it in front of her on the table.

DI BASCOMBE
I can tell you we currently have a suspect in custody -

JADE
Jamie. Yeah.

DI BASCOMBE
- but we do still need information - both on the murder weapon, which we still haven't found - and why the suspect did it -

DS FRANK
You were a good friend of Katie's, right?

JADE
Her best friend. Ask anyone.

DI BASCOMBE
Can you tell us about her.

JADE's lip curls, is this policing?

JADE
Ain't you got a kid in the school?

DI BASCOMBE doesn't like her mentioning Adam, but plays it with a smile.

DI BASCOMBE
Yes -

JADE
Adam, right? He's off. If you didn't know. Didn't get your cheekbones.

DI BASCOMBE
I don't see how -

JADE
Can you tell me about him?

DI BASCOMBE is put on the spot.

JADE (CONT'D)
Listen, all you need to know is...she's dead. She shouldn't

be. She got stabbed. She was the best person I knew. That's it.

DI BASCOMBE

Was Katie happy, Jade?

JADE

She didn't stab herself.

DS FRANK

What was her relationship with boys like?

JADE

You mean with Jamie? She weren't going anywhere near him.

DS FRANK

That's interesting. Did she dislike him, because we have Instagram posts from her which suggest they were friends?

JADE is beginning to boil.

JADE

You trying to blame her for all this, is that it?

DI BASCOMBE

No.

JADE

You got video. Everyone knows it. So why am I talking about Katie.

DI BASCOMBE

We're not asking you to talk bad about her...

JADE

You ARE! YOU ARE! I CAN HEAR IT IN ALL OF YOU!

MRS FENUMORE
Jade -

JADE takes a breath, she looks around the room - her pain cascading out of her. She forcibly cools herself down.

JADE
Can I go now, Lower School?

MRS FENUMORE
Bit of politeness.

JADE
I ain't feeling polite today. Can I go, Mrs Lower School?

DI BASCOMBE
Of course you can.

JADE
Thank you.

JADE stalks to the door and then she turns, she has tears in her eyes.

JADE (CONT'D)
You the best the blue got?

She slams out of the door.

DI BASCOMBE and DS FRANK look at each other. He smiles awkwardly, even though he doesn't feel like smiling.

He stands up and picks up his bag.

MRS FENUMORE
I'm so sorry, she's very upset.

INT. CORRIDOR. SCHOOL

They walk down the corridor. There are kids walking fast past them to lessons, many looking at their phones.

One kid runs fast towards them. He's carrying a set of football boots.

He swerves past, late for his lesson.

MRS FENUMORE
We'll start you in Eight-G. That's Jamie's class.

DI BASCOMBE
We know.

MRS FENUMORE
You've talked to some of the boys in the - Ryan and Tommy -

DI BASCOMBE
(harsh)
Does everyone think they know everything about this case?

Beat. He controls himself.

MRS FENUMORE
People are going to know more than you think all day.

They open the door and we enter before them.

INT. 8G'S CLASSROOM. SCHOOL

It's a noisy room. Things are going off a bit today.

When they see DI BASCOMBE and DS FRANK they calm down.

MRS FENUMORE
Where's Mr Malik?

DI BASCOMBE quickly scans the class, he sees RYAN sitting at the back. RYAN looks utterly petrified to see him again.

MORAY
Don't tell on Mr Malik, miss.

MRS FENUMORE
This is Detective Inspector Bascombe –

There's a couple of 'oooh's around the room and a few 'shut the fuck up's.

MRS FENUMORE (CONT'D)
He's got something to talk to you about.

DI BASCOMBE
Hi. As many of you know –

MRS FENUMORE interrupts.

MRS FENUMORE
Sorry. And this is Detective Sergeant Frank. Sorry.

She looks at DS FRANK, who shakes her head – it's not a problem.

MRS FENUMORE (CONT'D)
Sorry.

DI BASCOMBE
As many of you know there was a tragic incident the night before last that led to a fatality among your schoolmates.

MORAY
Did Jamie do it, sir? Really?

DI BASCOMBE is less comfortable here than in one-on-one situations.

MRS FENUMORE
Come on, shut up. Listen to the man.

MORAY
(laughing)
Oh shit. He did.

DI BASCOMBE
We have arrested someone but we are missing what we believe to be the murder weapon. I know that sounds very serious, but you might have the information we need, so we're asking you to come to us and talk to us if you need to.

MORAY
It true you got video?

MR MALIK enters the room, he's tucking in his shirt as he does. He notices the three adults at the front of the room, he takes a step back. This school is chaos.

DI BASCOMBE
If anyone wants to talk to us about any other issue connected to the case, then please -

MORAY
Mr Malik, we protected you -

MR MALIK
Hi. Hi. You must be the police.

MORAY
'You must be the police.' We love you, Mr Malik.

DI BASCOMBE
Mr Malik will pass on any names that come to him or you can just ring the station direct. It's Heywood Street and we're on 01632 960326.

He looks around to see if anyone is writing anything down. They're not.

DI BASCOMBE (CONT'D)
Please do talk to us. We're here.

He shoots a look at RYAN, who shrinks away.

DI BASCOMBE (CONT'D)
Okay.

He exits the room.

We stay in the room for a moment more.

MR MALIK
Okay. Let's get back to history shall we? I've got a film I want us to watch -

DS FRANK exits the room.

INT. CORRIDOR. SCHOOL

We go fast down the corridor, which is now empty of kids, and catch up to DI BASCOMBE walking alone.

We walk through a door which takes us to an exterior walkway, and carry on around the corner.

DI BASCOMBE takes an apple from his pocket. He takes a bite. He chews. He thinks. DS FRANK catches him up.

DS FRANK
Why do all schools smell the same? A mix of vomit, cabbage and wanking –

DI BASCOMBE
Sure.

DS FRANK
You really think we'll find the knife here?

DI BASCOMBE
Look, we may have enough, we may. But if we don't find the knife, he gets a bargaining chip – and we know he walked past the school where our CCTV is dark so...

DS FRANK
I get it.

DI BASCOMBE
And I want motive.

DS FRANK
I know you do.

DI BASCOMBE looks at DS FRANK, unsure of her position here.

DI BASCOMBE
I didn't understand that Jade girl –

DS FRANK
She was just upset.

DI BASCOMBE
She made it seem like Katie hated Jamie.

DS FRANK
It's going to be complicated whatever it was.

MRS FENUMORE catches them up. Together, they descend a flight of stairs.

MRS FENUMORE
Mr Malik's newly qualified.

DI BASCOMBE nods, he doesn't care about that.

MRS FENUMORE (CONT'D)
We did put a notice around you were coming. He's just - it's hard. The teachers are cut up by all this too.

DI BASCOMBE nods. He takes another bite of the apple.

They pass MR GARFIELD speaking to a STUDENT.

MR GARFIELD
Just tell me what you want here? You want me to send you to isolation? Is that it?

MRS FENUMORE
I taught her in Year Five. She was bright. Talked too much, but she could have been - she could have done something, that girl -

CARLA comes past them on the stairs, speaking into her phone.

CARLA
I got three girls hysterical in my office and he wants urgent first-aid training -

DS FRANK
It's a shock for everyone.

MRS FENUMORE
I think it's more than -

DI BASCOMBE
I want you to keep an eye on anyone who reacts funny - we'll trace them after school -

DS FRANK
Okay. If you're sure -

MRS FENUMORE
I can supply any names you like. Find their addresses for you too.

DI BASCOMBE
That could be useful.

MRS FENUMORE
Thank you. That's all I want to be. Just down here.

They walk on. We stop and look in through a window to a classroom where a video is being watched.

We travel on and see another classroom where a video is being watched.

In every classroom, a video is being watched.

No one is able to teach in this school.

DI BASCOMBE takes this in. His eyes registering the neglect.

We follow him through a set of doors, down the corridor, past a set of computer desks.

We stop at a set of lockers. One is open and has a picture of the moon on the inside of the door.

We plough on and enter the classroom - a classroom MRS FENUMORE, DI BASCOMBE and DS FRANK have just entered.

INT. 10G'S CLASSROOM. SCHOOL

DI BASCOMBE looks impatiently around the room, he knows this is his son's classroom.

MR CURTIS
Detective Inspector Bascombe is here to talk to you about what happened to Katie. He cares about this school, as many of you know he's also Adam's dad –

FREDO
Adam. Adam. Adam.

FREDO oinks. ADAM flinches. DI BASCOMBE looks at him apologetically. ADAM doesn't meet his eye.

MR CURTIS
That's enough.

FREDO continues to grunt. The class is laughing at him.

MR CURTIS (CONT'D)
I said stop that, Fredo.

FREDO carries on.

MR CURTIS (CONT'D)
I SAID STOP THAT!

DI BASCOMBE
I'm sure all of you are aware that a crime was committed two nights ago in our town. I am trying to understand why –

A fire alarm rings out.

DI BASCOMBE (CONT'D)
What?

MR CURTIS
Okay. Make an orderly line. We will PROCESS CALMLY BUT SWIFTLY

from the classroom onto the field.

DI BASCOMBE

A fire alarm?

MR CURTIS

No. Don't chat. Don't pack your things. If you want to take your bag you can. But you'll be coming back here afterwards –

We travel with the kids as they get into the orderly line. And then we travel past them into the corridor.

Which is full of kids behaving disorderly.

MR HUTCHINSON

You're supposed to be *filing* out of the school. Try and stay in straight lines...

BILLIE

Sir, you think it's terrorism, sir?

MR HUTCHINSON

No. Billie. It's not terrorism.

(to others)

No running. Stay in lines.

BILLIE

Seriously though, sir. First a murder, now a fire...

MR HUTCHINSON

If I see anyone running, it will be an immediate detention, do you hear me?

We travel past MR HUTCHINSON and out into the yard.

EXT. FOOTBALL FIELD. SCHOOL

We see the school amassing on the field. We pick out ADAM as he walks past us, alone, but in line.

We see RYAN looking incredibly scared.

We see DI BASCOMBE looking incredibly irritated.

MRS FENUMORE and DS FRANK walk behind him.

MRS FENUMORE
It'll be a false alarm.

DS FRANK says nothing.

MRS FENUMORE (CONT'D)
Though there was a fire last year. Someone threw a set of fireworks into the computer lab. Crowthers were selling ten for a quid, which didn't help.

DI BASCOMBE turns around. He's listening and appalled.

DS FRANK
Shit.

MRS FENUMORE
We contained the worst of it. Did you guys come - there were police who -

DI BASCOMBE sees MR MALIK and walks over to him through a group of kids looking self-conscious in PE kit.

DI BASCOMBE stands beside him and watches as someone else organises his class.

DI BASCOMBE
I read the reports - Jamie was a good student, right?

MR MALIK
Are we allowed to talk out here?

DI BASCOMBE
Yup. Did he show any sign of -
unhappiness -

MR MALIK has prickles coming out of him in all directions.

MR MALIK
I was just his tutor and history
teacher. You barely see them.

DI BASCOMBE nods.

MR MALIK (CONT'D)
They're all fucking impossible.

DI BASCOMBE looks at this slip of a teacher and nods.

We travel on through the yard.

GEORGIE
I can see smoke.

TAU
There ain't no smoke.

Suddenly, in the back of shot, JADE slaps RYAN hard around the back of the head.

JADE
What did you do? What did you do?

We travel fast to it, RYAN tries to protect himself, and she punches him hard in the face, and follows it up with one in his stomach. Her fury is unrelenting.

There's quickly a space and then a circle around them. Kids film it on their phones.

JADE (CONT'D)
You fucking freak. What did you do -

Teachers run in from all directions, including CARLA, the school nurse. DS FRANK runs too.

DI BASCOMBE stays back, watching everyone react, his sadness seeping through him.

JADE gets in one more fierce punch to the face. Blood starts to come out of his nose.

MR HUTCHINSON
Okay. Okay. Jade. Okay.

JADE
He's a fucking freak. He killed my friend.

MR HUTCHINSON
He didn't. He didn't.

RYAN
I didn't.

MRS BAILEY
Okay. Move away. Move away. MOVE AWAY.

She starts pushing kids back.

RYAN stays on the floor.

TOMMY is watching from a few steps away, but he takes a few more steps back.

DI BASCOMBE sees his son within the crowd. He tries to look at him with reassurance. ADAM shrinks back.

The alarm stops ringing. There's a collective sigh of indifference - at least that bit is over.

JADE is led into the building by MRS BAILEY.

DS FRANK tails RYAN as he's taken into the building by CARLA. MRS FENUMORE tails DS FRANK.

CARLA
Did you hit the back of your head? Did you land on it?

RYAN
Yeah.

MORAY
You just got banged by a girl, you sausage.

DI BASCOMBE takes one more look at ADAM, then looks around at TOMMY, and then follows them in.

INT. CORRIDOR. SCHOOL

He catches DS FRANK and MRS FENUMORE up as they walk carefully down the corridor. MRS FENUMORE leads them through the library.

MRS FENUMORE
We'll go back to Ten-G.

DI BASCOMBE
I'd like to talk to Ryan.

MRS FENUMORE
He'll be in with the nurse.

DI BASCOMBE
We'll join him.

MRS FENUMORE isn't at all sure. A look from DI BASCOMBE makes it clear she doesn't have much choice.

They see MORAY showing other kids his new rap video on his mobile phone.

MRS FENUMORE
Put that phone away, Moray, and get back to class.

MORAY
Shut up, miss.

MRS FENUMORE
Excuse me?

They carry on, swept up in the crowds of kids going back to their classes, dragging their feet, making drama.

She leads them to the nurse's suite.

INT. NURSE'S SUITE. SCHOOL

Where CARLA is already inspecting RYAN, a cold compress on his nose. DS FRANK and DI BASCOMBE stay a bit back.

CARLA
Do you remember losing consciousness?

RYAN
No.

CARLA
I'm pretty sure your nose isn't broken.

RYAN starts to cry.

CARLA (CONT'D)
Okay. Okay. Okay.

MR HUTCHINSON enters the room. He looks at RYAN and then at the detectives.

MR HUTCHINSON
Someone set the alarm off in the gym. Do you have everything you need?

DI BASCOMBE
Yes.

He nods. He looks at RYAN.

MR HUTCHINSON
Do we need to get him to casualty?

CARLA
Just working out whether he needs an HIA.

MR HUTCHINSON
Yes. Good good.

He exits. CARLA begins to check RYAN for a head injury.

DI BASCOMBE
I did want to talk to you, Ryan. Is now an okay time to do so?

RYAN
Okay.

DI BASCOMBE sits beside RYAN as the work continues to be done.

DI BASCOMBE
You might have a black eye, son.

RYAN
Yeah.

He can see the fear in RYAN. He smiles at him.

DI BASCOMBE
You know, when I was about your age, I once ran into a bus

shelter because I thought
I wanted a black eye.

RYAN

What?

DI BASCOMBE smiles.

DI BASCOMBE

I know. True story. Bit younger.
Lot younger. Maybe nine.

RYAN

Did it work?

DI BASCOMBE

(laughing)

I wanted to look like a cowboy.
Instead I knocked out a tooth and
looked like a – I don't know. And
it hurt.

RYAN smiles. DI BASCOMBE is pleased he does. He's trying everything to understand these kids and this situation.

DI BASCOMBE (CONT'D)

I look back now and I do – wonder
how my brain worked – I did loads
of things like that – it's crazy
what your brain tells you to do
when you're a kid.

RYAN

You were popular in school
though.

DI BASCOMBE

How do you work that out?

RYAN

You were.

DI BASCOMBE
I was. Once I got rid of the - my mum wouldn't let me cut my hair when I was younger. Once I shaved it, faded it. That was - things were better. Is that important to you? Popularity?

RYAN smiles at him, but it's a really uncertain smile.

RYAN
Course.

DI BASCOMBE
When we spoke to you -

RYAN
Tommy said you spoke to him 'n' all.

DI BASCOMBE
Yes.

RYAN
But his dad wouldn't let him say anything.

DI BASCOMBE
That's mostly - but not entirely right. Do you want your guardian here, Ryan?

RYAN
(no way)
No. Thank you. Were you *really* popular?

DI BASCOMBE isn't sure how to respond for a moment.

DI BASCOMBE
Yeah.

RYAN
With girls and...

DI BASCOMBE
I did okay.

RYAN
It doesn't look like you knocked out any teeth.

DI BASCOMBE
I did. This one here.

He points to one of his lower teeth.

RYAN
That a cap or a filling?

DI BASCOMBE
Filling.

RYAN
I got all my teeth. Brush 'em dead careful. I don't know why they matter so much. But they do.

There's a silence between them. DI BASCOMBE carefully analyses RYAN's face. RYAN notices him looking and turns away.

DI BASCOMBE
We are getting clearer on the geography of what happened that night. There are three things you could really help us with answers to...

RYAN
Okay.

DI BASCOMBE
What Jamie intended and what motivated – do you understand the word 'motivated'?

RYAN
Yeah. And 'intended'.

DI BASCOMBE
What motivated the - uh - why Jamie - did what he did. You can help with that.

RYAN nods. He wants to curl up inside his own brain. But he can't.

DI BASCOMBE (CONT'D)
Would you say - for instance - Jamie was happy or sad that night?

RYAN
I don't know. Normal.

DI BASCOMBE
Do you remember what you talked about?

RYAN
Nothing.

DI BASCOMBE
Did you ever talk about feelings with Jamie? I know it's not something mates really talk about -

RYAN
Yeah. No.

DI BASCOMBE
Can we talk about Katie?

RYAN
I don't know anything about her.

DI BASCOMBE
Can we talk about what Jamie said about Katie?

RYAN
I didn't know anything about what he was gonna do.

DI BASCOMBE nods.

DI BASCOMBE
Were they - would you describe them as friends?

RYAN
I don't think so. Not really. Like I say, I didn't really know her. Can I go? I don't like missing - lessons. I get - behind.

RYAN stands and makes for the door.

DI BASCOMBE
Can I ask you about the third thing I need, Ryan? Where the weapon might be - do you know of anywhere Jamie may have concealed it?

CARLA
Ryan, you've hit your head, you need to sit down -

RYAN
They keep saying if I don't - they keep saying they'll keep me back -

DI BASCOMBE
You don't want that.

RYAN nods. His face tears up again. He holds the tears back.

CARLA tries to hold him back but he's not having it.

We leave the room with RYAN.

We catch a glimpse of DI BASCOMBE's despairing face as we do.

INT. CORRIDOR. SCHOOL

RYAN travels along a corridor.

A mouse in a cat factory. He just wants to be small.

MR FRENCH (O.S.)
You will sit down. You will sit down. You will be silent. Not another word.

We travel past the classroom he's shouting in. RYAN looks in and then continues on.

We pick up the back of a harried teacher, who is carrying a load of books whilst texting, hurrying down the corridor.

INT. STAIRCASE. SCHOOL

We travel up a staircase. Following the teacher.

We walk past an empty languages classroom. We travel inside.

INT. EMPTY LANGUAGES CLASSROOM. SCHOOL

ALI THE TEACHER enters the classroom and lets MRS BAILEY know-

ALI (SA)
Jade's mum is on the way.

JADE is sat with MRS BAILEY.

She is silent.

JADE
Are you serious?

MRS BAILEY
Your mum needed to be told.

JADE
She'll be mad. She'll have to get out of work.

MRS BAILEY
How are you two - getting on together now?

JADE
It's - okay.

MRS BAILEY nods. JADE looks at her, insecure, she likes MRS BAILEY.

MRS BAILEY
I did say you might not be best coming in today.

JADE
Where you want me going? Mum don't like me in her house without her there, and I'm not walking round places she's - Katie's - been.

JADE almost breaks, but pulls herself back. She doesn't want to look weak.

JADE (CONT'D)
I'd go to her house. That's where I'd go.

MRS BAILEY
I'm sure her parents would love to -

JADE
Trust me. They wouldn't.

Beat. JADE computes everything.

JADE (CONT'D)
Am I in trouble?

MRS BAILEY
You know you are.

JADE
Will the police - ?

MRS BAILEY
I don't know. Depends what Ryan decides.

JADE
He's only a little boy.

MRS BAILEY
Then why did you do it?

JADE
I don't know.

MRS BAILEY nods.

MRS BAILEY
I know you're hurt, but you don't know that Ryan's got anything to do with what happened - Jade - please talk to me.

JADE starts to cry. It rises up inside like a torrent. She's irritated it does.

JADE
She was my best friend. She was the only one who thought I was okay. I don't have - I don't have - I don't know what - I don't have much else - I don't have no one else and -

MRS BAILEY
You do have other people, Jade -

JADE
I don't.

MRS BAILEY
You do, you've got lots of people -

JADE
You're just saying that.

MRS BAILEY
Jade, listen to me. But - but this loss - we are arranging for someone to -

JADE
Not another shrink -

MRS BAILEY
We are arranging for someone to -

JADE
No. No. Fuck that. No. NO.

She walks from the room.

MRS BAILEY
Where are you going? Jade. You're not allowed back to lessons - Jade -

INT. CORRIDOR. SCHOOL

We travel through the door, as JADE slams through it.

MRS BAILEY comes out to pursue her.

MRS BAILEY
Jade. You have to come -

JADE
Do I? DO I?

She slams past an anonymous kid standing at the end of the corridor.

It's ADAM.

His face alive with thoughts.

He looks around slightly furtively.

He walks a little way.

He sees a teacher coming. He walks the other way, and then down some stairs.

INT. STAIRCASE. SCHOOL

He walks quickly down the staircase.

INT. CORRIDOR. SCHOOL

He walks along the corridor. Looking in the window of every classroom, looking away if any teacher turns to notice him.

He stops when he sees what he's looking for. It's his dad...

DI BASCOMBE
What we are especially looking for is anything that anyone saw that night, or can give meaning to. If you can help us, we want to talk to you...

ADAM walks a little way away from the window. His dad is still not doing a great job of talking to kids.

After a beat, DI BASCOMBE, DS FRANK and MRS FENUMORE leave the room.

ADAM watches them for a moment, he sees his dad rub his face.

ADAM approaches and then lingers back, and then DI BASCOMBE sees him.

DI BASCOMBE (CONT'D)
Hi.

ADAM nods.

DI BASCOMBE (CONT'D)
Shouldn't you be in lessons?

ADAM
Yeah.

DI BASCOMBE waits - his son doesn't behave like this, there's something going on. But ADAM doesn't say anything.

DI BASCOMBE
You okay? You feeling sick again or something...

ADAM waits a beat more.

DI BASCOMBE signals for DS FRANK to take a step back.

ADAM
I just wanted - to - tell something to you -

DI BASCOMBE looks at him - what is this? But he goes with it. He nods.

He turns to MRS FENUMORE.

DI BASCOMBE
Can you find me somewhere to talk to Adam please?

MRS FENUMORE
Of course. Down here.

She walks down the corridor. ADAM walks reluctantly with them.

DS FRANK
Do you know what it's about? Do want me to come in with you?

DI BASCOMBE
No it's okay. I'll chat to him.

DS FRANK smiles at him.

INT. SMALL OFFICE. SCHOOL

ADAM enters the office and looks around.

DI BASCOMBE enters after him.

ADAM looks at a set of attendance reports pinned on the wall. This is awkward.

DI BASCOMBE
You okay? What was that about before?

ADAM
Yeah.

There's another silence. These two don't really have an open communication.

DI BASCOMBE
What did you want to - talk about -

ADAM
Just - uh - you said - you wanted to talk to people who might help you - understand -

DI BASCOMBE nods. He fidgets his fingers.

DI BASCOMBE
And you can - ? Help me?
Understand?

ADAM says nothing.

DI BASCOMBE waits, he takes a slightly yellowing apple from his pocket and resumes eating it.

ADAM
You don't think I can help -

DI BASCOMBE
No -

ADAM
- you want to go. I can tell.
Work or the gym. See you, Dad.

DI BASCOMBE
Fucking hell, Adam. If you've
got something to say...Is it the
knife? Has someone told you where
it is - because I got sniffer
dogs, people looking in drains -
and I do need to -

ADAM looks at his dad for one - two - three seconds. He's looking for sincerity. He decides to talk more.

ADAM
It's not going well because
you're not getting it.

DI BASCOMBE
What am I not getting?

ADAM
You're not reading what they're
doing. Insta - you've been
looking at Insta right?

DI BASCOMBE
Yes.

ADAM
Okay. So...

He takes his phone out. He scrolls through until he's on Instagram, he finds Jamie's page in a moment.

ADAM (CONT'D)
You seen what she wrote?

DI BASCOMBE
I have.

ADAM gets the comments up - Katie has written a dynamite stick followed by '100%' sign, same comment, picture after picture. He stops on one. It's been hearted fourteen times.

ADAM
Looks like she's being nice, right?

DI BASCOMBE
Isn't she?

ADAM
Dynamite - what did you think that means?

DI BASCOMBE doesn't know. ADAM sort of half-sneers, half-smiles at his dad. DI BASCOMBE reads it.

ADAM (CONT'D)
It's an exploding red pill - blue pill means you see the world as it wants you to, red pill - 'I see the truth' -

DI BASCOMBE
You guys watch *The Matrix*?

ADAM doesn't know what *The Matrix* is.

ADAM

What? What's that? No. I don't know. Red is truth - it's a call to action by the 'manosphere'.

DI BASCOMBE

The 'manosphere'?

ADAM

Which is where the one hundred comes into it. The eighty-twenty rule.

DI BASCOMBE

I don't know what that is either.

ADAM

Eighty per cent of women are attracted to twenty per cent of men. Women. You got to trick them 'cause you'll never get them in a normal way. Eighty per cent of women are - cut off or...She's saying he's an incel, Dad.

DI BASCOMBE takes a moment.

DI BASCOMBE

But he's thirteen. You can't be involuntarily celibate at thirteen.

ADAM

I know.

DI BASCOMBE

Who's not celibate at thirteen?

ADAM

She's saying he always will be. That's what they say - you're an incel - a virgin forever - and all those people have hearted it which means they agree. With her.

DI BASCOMBE looks at the page again. No. Is this right?

DI BASCOMBE
So – this is bullying? It feels like a reach –

ADAM'S face falls.

ADAM
Don't believe me then.

ADAM makes to exit. His face burning.

DI BASCOMBE
No. No. Adam. Please. This is useful. Please.

ADAM stops.

DI BASCOMBE (CONT'D)
Just – all that from two symbols?

ADAM
You text hearts right, to Mum?

DI BASCOMBE smiles softly.

DI BASCOMBE
Only when I can't think of something to say.

ADAM
What colour?

DI BASCOMBE
Red.

ADAM
Means love. Purple means horny. Yellow – I'm interested, you interested?

DI BASCOMBE
Right. Really...

ADAM

Pink - I'm interested, but not in sex. Orange - you're going to be fine. It all - all of it has meaning - everything - has meaning -

DI BASCOMBE

Good job I send red, really.

ADAM

I could show you fifteen others - comments sent to Jamie. All different emojis. All saying the same thing.

Beat. This is huge, and hugely confusing.

DI BASCOMBE

And Katie was - leading it - in relation to Jamie? This incel bullying?

ADAM

I don't know. They're two years below. That's just - this is just what I'm seeing, you know?

Beat. DI BASCOMBE thinks.

DI BASCOMBE

I can't tell you what he did -

ADAM

We all know what he did. I just thought you needed to - it was just - embarrassing watching you - blunder about.

DI BASCOMBE nods. He's used to his son calling him embarrassing.

ADAM (CONT'D)

Sorry.

DI BASCOMBE half-smiles, half-nods, but he's worried.

DI BASCOMBE
No. Don't be – I don't like blundering –

Beat. He looks at his son, full of worry.

DI BASCOMBE (CONT'D)
Does any of this Instagram stuff affect you?

ADAM
(no no no)
It's not about me.

DI BASCOMBE
But does it, son?

ADAM looks up, burnt slightly.

ADAM
You don't call me 'son' – you call other people 'son' – you don't call me 'son' –

DI BASCOMBE
Sorry.

Beat. A burnt pause.

ADAM
No, I'm on Insta – but I don't post.

DI BASCOMBE nods.

DI BASCOMBE
And are you okay?

ADAM
(no)
Yeah.

There is a desperate pause.

DI BASCOMBE looks at his son and his need to say 'I love you' sort of drifts in the air, but it can't be said aloud.

DI BASCOMBE
(I love you)
I really - appreciate this, Adam. Thank - you.

ADAM
Yeah. Okay. I should get back to the last bit of class.

ADAM thinks, blinks and exits.

DI BASCOMBE stays still a moment.

INT. CORRIDOR. SCHOOL

We travel with ADAM as he strides - and he really is trying to stride - back to class.

He walks past DS FRANK and MRS FENUMORE.

He doesn't look at either of them. He wants the world to swallow him up. But then he generally wants the world to swallow him up.

DI BASCOMBE joins them. DS FRANK looks at DI BASCOMBE - was that useful?

DI BASCOMBE nods at her.

DI BASCOMBE
We've been - reading the Instagram stuff wrong -

DS FRANK
Oh.

DI BASCOMBE
She was bullying him. Incel stuff. You know what that is?

DS FRANK
Right.

MRS FENUMORE
I don't. What is that?

DS FRANK
Involuntary celibate. The – Andrew Tate stuff.

MRS FENUMORE
Oh. Yes. Well, I've heard of him.

DI BASCOMBE rubs his face, he's thinking, deeply thinking.

DI BASCOMBE
Thanks for your time Mrs Fenumore.

MRS FENUMORE
Sorry?

DI BASCOMBE
We don't need anything more from you today, thanks for your time. You've been incredibly useful.

MRS FENUMORE looks at DI BASCOMBE and then DS FRANK.

MRS FENUMORE
It was nice to be useful. I'll be in reception if you need me.

She walks away. Back to her lessons. She looks reluctantly back.

DI BASCOMBE leans against the wall, suddenly knackered.

DI BASCOMBE
I hate this place.

DS FRANK
Alright, drama. We're only here because of you.

DI BASCOMBE
You think anyone's learning anything here? It's a holding pen for - shit.

DS FRANK
That's harsh.

DI BASCOMBE
Videos in every lesson, teachers just - and you're the one who says it smells bad -

DS FRANK
There'll be some good teachers. Some good students. My school was a bit like this.

DI BASCOMBE
How did you survive?

DS FRANK
Mrs Benton. She taught art. I was - I liked drawing and - taking photographs. All kids really need is one thing makes 'em feel okay about themselves.

DI BASCOMBE looks at her for a beat, trying to figure her out.

DI BASCOMBE
You want kids?

DS FRANK looks at him, surprised.

DS FRANK
You know - you have never asked me that question.

DI BASCOMBE
Sort of thing we're not allowed to ask any more, right?

DS FRANK
You're allowed to ask friends. And no, not really.

DI BASCOMBE
I never wanted them.

Beat. He rubs his face again.

DI BASCOMBE (CONT'D)
But I - love him very very much.

And that truth is almost painful.

DS FRANK
Is he okay?

DI BASCOMBE
He just - said more to me than he has in a really long time and -

DS FRANK
That's a good thing isn't it?

DI BASCOMBE
I don't...The thing is, I'm not always the best fit - as a dad - for him.

DS FRANK
I'm sure you can be.

Beat. She looks at him. She sees his soul for a moment. She knows they need to switch away.

DI BASCOMBE
We still don't have the knife. But this - feels - like -

DS FRANK
We can go back to the station? Thank fuck for that.

DI BASCOMBE

You've hated being here all day, haven't you?

DS FRANK

You know the thing I don't like about our job? The line is always 'a man raped a woman', the perpetrator is always given the front line. Katie isn't important, Jamie is. We just spent the day following his - brain around and I just... Everyone will always remember his name, no one hers.

DI BASCOMBE

It's our job to understand why this happened.

DS FRANK

You really think you can ever know? We got video. We know what he did. Why - I don't need.

DS FRANK looks at him searchingly for a moment.

DI BASCOMBE

Go back to the station if you want - I want to talk to Ryan one last time.

DS FRANK

Ryan?

DI BASCOMBE

Last one, I promise.

DS FRANK

Come on then, mate.

They walk down the corridor. We watch them go.

The school seems somehow calmer now.

As we look through into the classrooms. Somehow there's a bit more hope in them.

We stop and watch a maths lesson where the teacher is making her students really laugh.

Then we turn and we race to catch DI BASCOMBE and DS FRANK up.

INT. 8G'S CLASSROOM. SCHOOL

The class is watching a boring film about the build-up to the Industrial Revolution.

DI BASCOMBE knocks, and then enters the classroom. MR MALIK looks up from where he's been sitting doing nothing.

The class are instantly alert to have the police back. We look particularly at the scared, bruised face of RYAN.

DI BASCOMBE

Sorry to bother you again, Mr Malik.

MR MALIK

No. No. Not at all. How can we help?

RYAN inches open the window.

MORAY

Stop the tape Mr Malik. We're just getting to the good bit I think.

MR MALIK

Thanks - Moray.

MR MALIK turns off the TV. DI BASCOMBE looks around and sees a few of the students asleep.

DI BASCOMBE
I need to speak to Ryan again.

Suddenly RYAN opens the window and flips himself out the other side.

DI BASCOMBE (CONT'D)
No. No.

MORAY
Holy shit.

DI BASCOMBE
Ryan - stop -

RYAN runs across the quad.

MORAY
Holy shit.

MR MALIK
Okay. Settle down.

DI BASCOMBE follows RYAN to the window and awkwardly climbs through after him. He runs across the quad.

MORAY
It's a police chase. But it's a crap one.

DS FRANK bolts out of the room and goes the other way.

We travel through the window after DI BASCOMBE.

And follow him as he runs desperately after RYAN.

EXT. QUAD. SCHOOL

RYAN bolts out of the quad, and round the side of the school.

DI BASCOMBE is in good condition, but not great condition.

He can run, but he neither has the desperation nor the fitness of RYAN.

However, he is determined, and won't give this up easily.

RYAN dashes down a small walkway.

EXT. WALKWAY. SCHOOL

He looks back. DI BASCOMBE is getting closer to him.

DI BASCOMBE is pushing as hard as he can.

RYAN runs through and grabs the school gate, trying to slam it shut behind him.

But DI BASCOMBE catches the gate, RYAN lets go and sprints down the pavement.

We stay with DI BASCOMBE - a few steps behind - as he runs.

EXT. STREET

He watches RYAN run out of the school and straight across the street. It's a horrifying moment.

He runs straight into the traffic.

A car brakes hard and beeps loudly.

But RYAN doesn't give a shit.

DI BASCOMBE gets out his warrant card as he runs.

He holds his warrant card high as he runs across the road after RYAN.

RYAN looks back, his face now petrified. Why can't he shake this man?

DI BASCOMBE reads the fear.

DI BASCOMBE
I'm going to - I know where you live, son - come on, Ryan -

EXT. ALLEYWAY

RYAN runs into an alleyway on the other side of the school.

He realises it's a dead end.

He looks around for a possible way out. There is none.

He reaches the dead end and tries to scale the fence. But he can't get any sort of grip.

He turns to run back, but DI BASCOMBE is too close.

He stops.

He breathes out.

He waits. Shit.

DI BASCOMBE - breathing deeply - can't talk for a moment.

RYAN just looks at him.

DI BASCOMBE
What are you doing?

DI BASCOMBE takes another beat. He wipes his forehead. He feels sick.

DI BASCOMBE (CONT'D)
What does 'incel' mean to you?

RYAN
What?

DI BASCOMBE
What - does the word - 'incel' - mean to - you?

DI BASCOMBE looks at him carefully.

DI BASCOMBE (CONT'D)
Katie.

DI BASCOMBE wipes his forehead.

DI BASCOMBE (CONT'D)
She called Jamie an 'incel'?

RYAN
Who d'you hear that off?

DI BASCOMBE
Did she?

RYAN
I - ain't talking to you.

DI BASCOMBE
Ryan, was Katie bullying -

RYAN
Why are you always talking to me - why are you never talking to Tommy?

In the background, DS FRANK drives up to the entrance of the alleyway in a car.

She parks the car, blocking the way out of the alleyway.

She gets out.

DI BASCOMBE
Tommy doesn't - talk as openly as you.

RYAN
So you're picking on me because
I say stuff?

DI BASCOMBE
And I don't think Tommy knew
Jamie like you did.

RYAN looks up at him, he hates that he's right. DS FRANK approaches them both.

RYAN
I knew that stuff about bus stops
was bullshit.

DI BASCOMBE
It wasn't. Tell me what you know
about how Jamie and Katie -

RYAN
I don't know much.

DI BASCOMBE
Did Jamie hate her for what she
put on Instagram?

RYAN
No. I hated her. He was more -
scared of her.

Beat. DI BASCOMBE digests this.

RYAN (CONT'D)
It wasn't like we weren't bullied
before. But we - mostly weren't -
noticed. And then she - uh - she
started - suddenly we were all
everyone was talking about -

DI BASCOMBE
Saying you were 'incels'?

RYAN
Just him. But we were with him.
Always.

DI BASCOMBE looks at RYAN carefully.

RYAN (CONT'D)
I didn't know - if I knew he was going to do that I'd have -

DI BASCOMBE
Stopped him?

RYAN
I thought he'd just scare her -

DI BASCOMBE
Did you help him get the knife, Ryan?

RYAN
No. No. It was - was - my knife.

These are huge words. RYAN is shocked he's saying them.

RYAN (CONT'D)
I just - wanted things the way they were - it wasn't my fault.

DI BASCOMBE
Do you know where the knife is now?

RYAN
No. He didn't give it back.

DI BASCOMBE nods at DS FRANK.

DS FRANK
Ryan Kowalska, the time is three-twenty-one p.m., I am arresting you on suspicion of conspiracy to murder.

RYAN
What? No. It wasn't a weapon. It was just from the kitchen -

DS FRANK
You do not have to say anything. But, it may harm your defence if -

RYAN
What?

DS FRANK
- if you do not mention when questioned something which you later rely on in court. Anything you do say may be given in evidence.

RYAN numbly nods and is led to the car.

DI BASCOMBE
You okay doing this alone?

DS FRANK
(surprised)
Yeah.

RYAN
(this is important)
You weren't lying were you - about knocking out your tooth?

DI BASCOMBE
No.

He is placed into the car. DS FRANK moves to get into the front.

DI BASCOMBE (CONT'D)
Get him processed. Notify everyone that needs to...

DS FRANK
Of course.

DI BASCOMBE makes a decision.

DI BASCOMBE
And charge Jamie.

DS FRANK
Without you?

DI BASCOMBE
We got all we need now.

DS FRANK
We still haven't got the knife.

DI BASCOMBE
I know. But I've got to sort - there's something I've got to sort -

DS FRANK
Are you okay?

DI BASCOMBE
Yeah.

DS FRANK nods at him, softly smiles, and gets in the car.

DI BASCOMBE stands for a moment in the street.

Watching them leave.

Then he turns.

He walks back towards the school, back through the gates.

EXT. SCHOOL / INT. DI BASCOMBE'S CAR

DI BASCOMBE gets into his car. He sits heavily in the front seat. The door open to let the air in.

He looks tired. He looks unwell. He looks - disappointed somehow.

He looks around for some water. He doesn't have any water. There's an apple in his glovebox though. He takes it out - every inch of him not wanting to bite - but he does bite - he starts to eat it.

The bell rings inside the school and children start to pile out.

He gets into his car fully now and closes the door.

He watches them as they stream past.

He watches MR MALIK as he runs to his car and gets inside. Desperate to leave.

He guns his car into life immediately and beeps a kid that gets in the way as he drives away.

And then DI BASCOMBE sees his own child.

Sees ADAM, walking in that slightly lopsided way, coming out of the school.

He studies him for a moment.

And then winds down his window.

DI BASCOMBE

Adam? Adam.

ADAM looks at his dad and then walks slowly towards him.

ADAM

I don't want a lift home. I take the bus.

DI BASCOMBE makes a decision and gets out of the car.

DI BASCOMBE

No. I know. I just - wondered if you - I wasn't going to go home. I'm hungry. I just wondered if you fancied going for chips and a - can of Coke or something?

ADAM looks at his dad for a long time.

ADAM
You've got your case.

DI BASCOMBE
We're close to passing it on, to be honest, and I'm - allowed a little time off. I just thought - I just would like to -

He hesitates.

DI BASCOMBE (CONT'D)
I'm trying here.

ADAM is unsure what this invitation means, but he decides to go with it.

ADAM
Yeah. I can be hungry.

DI BASCOMBE
Good. Thank you.

DI BASCOMBE gets back in the car.

ADAM hesitates and then gets in the car. We follow him in.

ADAM
Okay?

DI BASCOMBE
Yeah. What d'you have today? Lessons I mean...

ADAM
Maths. Chemistry. French.

DI BASCOMBE
They good? You - like them?

ADAM
I like chemistry. Some bits anyway.

DI BASCOMBE
What 'bits' are the 'bits' you like?

ADAM
We did an experiment today about the reactivity of metals.

DI BASCOMBE
(laughing)
You already lost me.

Beat. He realises that might have been the wrong thing to say.

DI BASCOMBE (CONT'D)
Chips then.

ADAM
The Chinese place on Chapel Hill.

DI BASCOMBE
A Chinese for chips?

ADAM
Honestly. I'm not lying. They're the best.

DI BASCOMBE smiles.

DI BASCOMBE
Let's go there then.

He starts the car.

And we watch the car drive away.

And we stay steady, watching kids walk past.

And then JADE walks past us.

And we walk with JADE.

Her heavy footsteps leading us away.

She stops - as if unsure which way to go - and we travel around her to look at her face.

We see the loss on it.

And it hurts.

And then she walks on. And we watch the faces of kids as they continue to file past.

We see all sorts on their faces – the hope-despair axis on full display.

And then we see phones start to come out. There are phones suddenly everywhere. Blooming like spring flowers all over the place.

And we take off. We start to fly.

We watch the absorption. The total absorption.

Looking down, as if looking for clues.

We pass over the town. Fly over it. Seeing all the intricate ways it has lived and survived.

It feels small and yet shuddering under the weight of what's happened here.

We pause only when we reach –

EXT. CAR PARK. CROWTHERS

The car park where the incident happened.

The car park where Katie was killed.

And there's a police ribbon tied up, twisting in the wind.

And there's piles of flowers and piles of teddies.

And it's almost like we have a moment of grace.

A moment of memory.

And

it's

almost

like

shadows

pass

across

it.

And then - we see EDDIE get out of his van. A bouquet in his hand.

He adds it to the pile.

CREDITS.

Matthew Lewis (Director of Photography) filming Luke Charnley in Episode One, courtesy of Ben Blackall/Netflix © 2024

Stephen Graham (as Eddie Miller) in Episode One, courtesy of Netflix © 2024

Left to right: Ashley Sinani (1st Assistant Sound), Matthew Lewis, Faye Marsay (as DS Misha Frank), Ashley Walters (as DI Luke Bascombe), Owen Cooper (as Jamie Miller) and Stephen Graham in Episode One, courtesy of Netflix © 2024

Matthew Lewis filming Ashley Walters and Faye Marsay in Episode Two, courtesy of Ben Blackall/Netflix © 2024

Amari Bacchus (as Adam Bascombe) and Ashley Walters in Episode Two, courtesy of Ben Blackall/Netflix © 2024

Matthew Lewis launching the drone shot in Episode Two, courtesy of Netflix © 2024

Erin Doherty (as Briony Ariston) in Episode Three, courtesy of Ben Blackall/Netflix © 2024

Director Philip Barantini rehearsing Owen Cooper and Erin Doherty in Episode Three, courtesy of Netflix © 2024

Filming Owen Cooper and Erin Doherty in Episode Three, courtesy of Ben Blackall/Netflix © 2024

Filming Stephen Graham in Episode Four, courtesy of Netflix © 2024

Filming Stephen Graham driving Eddie's van in Episode Four, courtesy of Netflix © 2024

Christine Tremarco (as Manda Miller) and Stephen Graham in Episode Four, courtesy of Ben Blackall/Netflix © 2024

EPISODE THREE

Erin Doherty (as Briony Ariston), courtesy of Netflix © 2024

SEVEN MONTHS

INT. RECEPTION. STANDLING SECURE TRAINING CENTRE

BRIONY, thirty, professional, demurely dressed, is in a secure area.

BRIONY

Hi.

RECEPTION

Back again? Sign in please.

A photo is taken on a mini camera.

BRIONY deposits her phone, her keys, her gum and a rape alarm into a metal drawer.

She opens her handbag – we see a cling-film-wrapped sandwich, a Tupperware of mini marshmallows, a notebook, and a paper file inside – and pats down her pockets to make sure that's everything.

The drawer is closed and someone retrieves all the objects on the other side. They are put into a bag.

BRIONY

Okay?

RECEPTION

Yes, love.

He slides underneath an ID badge. She walks through a metal detector and passes green.

She stands by a big door. There's a huge buzz and then it's opened.

INT. CORRIDOR. STANDLING SECURE TRAINING CENTRE

She walks down a corridor and up to a lift.

She looks up again at the camera, holding up her pass. The lift doors open.

She walks into the lift. She presses '2'.

A man – coming from another door – hurries to get in the lift beside her. He presses '3'.

CHARLIE
You don't work here?

BRIONY
I'm a visitor.

She shows her pass ID, it says 'BRIONY ARISTON, CLINICAL PSYCHOLOGIST'.

CHARLIE
Right.

The doors open. She walks out without looking back.

INT. LOBBY. 2ND FLOOR. STANDLING SECURE TRAINING CENTRE

VICTOR is waiting for her.

VICTOR
Right – do you want to just come through for a sec?

She's ushered in and through to Victor's office.

BRIONY
Sorry I'm a bit late.

INT. OFFICE. STANDLING SECURE TRAINING CENTRE

There is a bank of CCTV screens which VICTOR has been monitoring.

VICTOR
That's alright. I saw you coming up on the cameras. He's being brought down.

BRIONY
I heard he was involved in a violent incident.

VICTOR
How d'you hear that?

BRIONY
It was reported up. It'd be useful to see it -

VICTOR
Is it relevant to what you'll - uh assess?

BRIONY
I'd like to see it.

VICTOR
Okay. I'll heat up the megaport.

VICTOR goes to a computer and begins flicking through various files.

BRIONY looks up at the CCTV screens and flicks between them. On one a session is happening with eight kids sat in a circle, on another two kids sit drawing together, on another a group of kids are watching TV, and on one she sees JAMIE's face vividly framed.

He's being brought through a security door by a big bloke called FRANK.

VICTOR (CONT'D)
He's been pretty quiet.

BRIONY
Yeah.

VICTOR
If that's relevant - if what I think - observe - is relevant to what you assess.

BRIONY says nothing.

VICTOR finds the file.

VICTOR (CONT'D)
And here we go -

We watch JAMIE fighting with another kid. It gets quite violent between them. But it's quite equal, both are getting blows in.

VICTOR (CONT'D)
It was just bruising and scratching.

BRIONY
I read the report.

VICTOR
Both blamed the other.

BRIONY
I know. I read the report.

VICTOR
You're on what? Five visits?

BRIONY
Yes.

VICTOR
Do you know what you're going to say in the report?

BRIONY
I wouldn't be here if I knew that.

VICTOR
The other one - the other one of you - only needed three -

BRIONY
Please don't say any more. It's important I know nothing of what the other psychologist - says, does or thinks.

VICTOR smiles. BRIONY looks back at the CCTV screens. JAMIE is no longer on them. She scans across them.

BRIONY (CONT'D)
It's about making the right assessment, not the fastest assessment.

VICTOR
Sorry, I'm just being an idiot.

BRIONY
No. Just the way I work.

A green button suddenly flashes.

VICTOR
Right - that's Jamie in place.

BRIONY nods.

VICTOR (CONT'D)
I'll take you through.

BRIONY
I need to get a hot chocolate from the machine.

VICTOR
I remember.

He nods and presses a button to release the door.

INT. CORRIDOR. STANDLING SECURE TRAINING CENTRE

They walk to a drinks machine. BRIONY pushes a button. Hot chocolate starts to pour.

There's the sudden sound of a scream, she turns towards it.

VICTOR
Got a torture lab in the basement. Government-approved. All very hush-hush.

BRIONY takes the Tupperware from her handbag. She empties the mini marshmallows into the hot chocolate. This is very deliberate. VICTOR frowns as he watches her.

VICTOR (CONT'D)
What are they?

BRIONY
He likes his hot chocolate with marshmallows on.

VICTOR
You must mean business. You never did them before.

BRIONY says nothing. A siren blares. VICTOR listens to it.

VICTOR (CONT'D)
Mark I think. I can tell who they are by their screams now. Twelve. Abused by his mother quite brutally. Radiator burns all over him. Poor kid. Don't know what he did to get here. He's not famous like your Jamie.

Two CARE WORKERS come rushing past.

VICTOR (CONT'D)
Come on! Move it!

She nods - she's used to VICTOR - she walks towards the door. VICTOR inputs a code and the door swings open with a buzz.

INT. VISITOR ROOM. STANDLING SECURE TRAINING CENTRE

This is quite a large room, made for quite a few people. The room is multipurpose. There's board games and balls - all locked away - but it doesn't smell of prison.

There is one table in the middle, which has JAMIE sat at it. FRANK is stood behind him.

BRIONY smiles as she approaches JAMIE. He half-smiles back. She's immediately warmer with him than we've seen her with anyone previously.

FRANK
You okay?

BRIONY
Yes. Hi Jamie.

JAMIE
Hi.

FRANK
You need us, we're here.

BRIONY
Yes.

FRANK
Same goes for you, Jamie.

JAMIE
I know.

FRANK
We'll be watching, okay, Jamie?

JAMIE nods.

FRANK exits the room with VICTOR just behind him.

BRIONY puts down the hot chocolate. She smiles again.

BRIONY
Hot chocolate. Lots of sprinkles.

JAMIE
You remembered? Thanks.

She pushes the hot chocolate across the table to him. He touches the sprinkles.

BRIONY
And I saved you half my sandwich in case you were hungry.

She takes the cling-film-wrapped sandwich out of her bag.

JAMIE
What is it?

BRIONY
Cheese and pickle.

JAMIE
No tomatoes?

BRIONY
Tomatoes don't go very well with pickle.

JAMIE
(hopeful)
No salad?

She unwraps the cling film – laughing.

BRIONY
Would I do that to you? No tomatoes, no salad. Just cheese and pickle. Do you want it? I'll save it for later.

JAMIE
I'll have it. Not sure about the pickle but I'll have it.

She passes it across to him. She's wary but she likes him.

JAMIE (CONT'D)
Did you make it?

BRIONY
Yeah.

JAMIE
You make butties do you?

BRIONY
You think that's weird?

JAMIE
Yeah. No. My mum makes butties.

BRIONY
(smiling)
That makes two of us then.

Beat. He drinks the hot chocolate.

JAMIE
This is good.

BRIONY
Careful. It's a bit hot -

JAMIE
I don't mind hot.

Beat.

BRIONY
You're looking better than last time.

JAMIE
What does that mean?

BRIONY
You've got some of your colour back.

JAMIE
(grinning)
You sound like a granny.

BRIONY
Do I?

JAMIE
'Oh, you got your colour back, Jamie. You can't have been that ill.'

BRIONY
(laughing)
That's a good voice.

JAMIE
No.

Beat.

BRIONY
Do you see your grandparents much?

JAMIE
(sardonic)
Not recently.

BRIONY
No, I meant before - all this.

JAMIE
No. A bit. My dad's - side. My mum - don't get on with hers.

BRIONY
Yes, of course, we talked about that. What's your dad's mum and dad like?

JAMIE
I don't know. Like him.

BRIONY
What does that mean?

JAMIE
They like things as they like them. 'No gravy? Such a shame' or 'I like a slice with my dinner if you've got one in, Amanda.'

BRIONY
Slice of what?

JAMIE
Bread. You're posh aren't you?

BRIONY
No. I'm just - not from where you're from.

JAMIE
What do you call bread? If you don't call it a slice -

BRIONY
(smiling)
Um. Bread.

JAMIE
You're posh.

BRIONY laughs again.

BRIONY
If it makes you - happy that I am - then I am.

JAMIE
What do you call your grandad? Bet you call him Grandpa?

BRIONY
I do not.

JAMIE
Bet you do.

BRIONY
I call him - Poppop.

JAMIE
Poppop??

They both laugh. She knows how it sounds.

BRIONY
I do. Yes.

JAMIE
'Poppop' - really?

BRIONY
Yes.

JAMIE
Jesus - I've not heard that one before.

BRIONY
Okay.

She laughs.

JAMIE
You're *really* posh.

BRIONY
I don't know why I call him that. Maybe he asked me to. You not gonna eat your sandwich?

JAMIE
I'll eat it later. It's just the pickle. I hate it.

She smiles and she looks at him carefully.

BRIONY
You hate it? I really messed up then. So can we talk about you - you see a lot of your dad in your grandad, do you?

JAMIE
Yeah. I don't know.

BRIONY
Is it just what they say - or how they do things? What's your dad and his dad like?

JAMIE knows she's getting serious now. He smiles, trying to deflect her.

JAMIE
Um. Men?

BRIONY
Does that mean - are they quite - is 'masculine' an okay word to use?

JAMIE
You used it.

BRIONY
Now when I hear the word masculine, I think: They can mend things. They like making things. They like sport. They like going to the pub.

JAMIE
Yeah. Not the pub. But yeah.

BRIONY
Your dad doesn't go to the pub?

JAMIE
Not really. A bit. Not as much as my poppop does.

BRIONY
(laughing)
You're not going to let me forget that are you? So your grandad's more of a pub man is he?

JAMIE
(what?)
I don't know. He's not round *that* much. Grandad.

BRIONY
How much?

JAMIE
Uh. You really want to...Every other Sunday maybe. Sometimes in the week. To look after us if they're both - Mum and Dad are both working. But that's more Granny. Bit more in the holidays. We went to Tenerife with them once.

BRIONY
On holiday?

JAMIE
(dry)
No. Banana picking.

BRIONY smiles. We see she's working towards something.

JAMIE (CONT'D)
Obviously it was on holiday.

BRIONY laughs.

BRIONY
Okay. If I was also - thinking about masculine - men - the other thing I'd think about in relation to masculine men is how they -

JAMIE
This all started cos I said you sounded like a granny.

BRIONY
What?

He's noticed she's driving towards something. JAMIE notices things.

JAMIE
This all started *because* I said you sounded like a granny. Now you're going on about 'masculine' stuff.

BRIONY
Yes.

JAMIE
First time you came you had actual questions – 'Is this right, Jamie? Do you know whether this is wrong, Jamie?' Now you just chat shit.

BRIONY
I hope I don't.

JAMIE
First time you're all 'If an adult guinea pig eats one of its kids, is that normal or weird?' Now you're – 'What do you call bread?'

BRIONY
Come on. I'm just – interested in your dad and your grandad.

JAMIE
Cos this all – feels like a trick so...

BRIONY
A trick? A trick into what?

JAMIE
My dad's okay, alright?

BRIONY
Yes. Yes. I know.

JAMIE
Just - talking about him - there isn't a need -

BRIONY
Okay. If that's how you feel. But I'm not tricking you.

There's a silence.

JAMIE
And now I've pissed you off.

BRIONY
No.

JAMIE
Can I see - what you got written down about me?

BRIONY
(smiling)
Do you see me writing anything down?

JAMIE
You must write stuff down.

BRIONY
Yes.

JAMIE
Can I see what you wrote - you've written?

BRIONY
Of course you can't.

JAMIE
Dillon - and the other lawyers - they say you work for us.

BRIONY
That isn't what they say and I know that because I asked them

the last time you said that to me.

JAMIE
You talk to them?

BRIONY
I've explained this, Jamie, I've been employed by your team, but I don't work for you.

JAMIE
What do you tell them?

BRIONY
I am writing an independent – that's a really important word here –

JAMIE
What do they say to you?

BRIONY
– an independent pre-sentence offence report – which the judge will read in order to get an understanding of you and your understanding of the charges, okay?

There's a silence.

BRIONY (CONT'D)
All I want to do – is talk to you, Jamie, and have you talk to me. Like you say, I've asked some straightforward questions. But I think – you – and everyone else in fact – are more complicated than straightforward – questions allow for. We had a good conversation last time. Can't we try that again?

JAMIE sits back, unsure for a moment. And then grudgingly leans in again.

JAMIE
What did we talk about last time?

BRIONY
Your sister. Your mum. Your friends. We went all over the place. Just like this time.

JAMIE
Can't remember saying much about them.

BRIONY
You did. And how you felt about them. How well Lisa does, what you think your mum thinks of you. That sort of thing.

JAMIE
And now you want to talk about Dad?

BRIONY
I want to talk about lots of things. I can tell you what I wrote down - the questions I wrote down to talk to you about today - if that helps?

JAMIE
Yes.

BRIONY
I wrote about - well, I wanted to talk about the fight you had -

JAMIE
That was nothing.

BRIONY
I was interested why you got in a fight -

JAMIE
He actually hit me first.

BRIONY
Why?

JAMIE
We've had beef. Over - stuff. It doesn't really matter. It wasn't a proper fight.

BRIONY
You're telling me it's not that interesting?

JAMIE
Yeah.

BRIONY
Okay. Let's move on.

JAMIE
(grinning)
I'm in charge now am I?

BRIONY
And I wrote that I wanted to talk to you about what being a man feels like -

JAMIE
(laughing)
You want a cock and balls?

BRIONY
No. I'm interested - in what being a man feels like - for you -

JAMIE is immediately a bit concerned.

JAMIE
I don't know.

BRIONY
Too big a question, right? And the fight is too small a question. And that's why - you see - it's more useful - for me - to see where the conversation goes and steer it a bit - into - for instance - what you think of your dad and grandad - and what kind of men you think they are - rather than saying - 'So, Jamie, what do you think being a man feels like?'

JAMIE half-laughs.

JAMIE
(posh voice)
'So, Jamie, what do you think being a man feels like?'

BRIONY
It's not a trick. Just a conversation. Like I say. So do you think it's okay - to talk about your dad... a bit...

JAMIE considers the question.

JAMIE
Can't I see your notes - what you wrote? How you wrote it?

BRIONY
(smiling)
No. You're not that in charge. Does your dad like his job?

JAMIE
He fixes toilets, what d'you think? He works hard. Long hours. You get the best money for emergency plumbing out-of-hours, you know?

BRIONY
Is he funny?

JAMIE
Sometimes.

BRIONY
Loving?

JAMIE
No. That'd be weird.

BRIONY
Angry?

JAMIE takes a beat.

JAMIE
I - suppose.

BRIONY
How angry does he get?

JAMIE
He's never hit me.

BRIONY
Okay. Go on.

JAMIE
Go on, what? Is that what this is about?

BRIONY
Why do you call him angry?

JAMIE
He just gets mad - we all do -

BRIONY
So he's just angry - he's just angry in a normal way -

JAMIE thinks. BRIONY watches him carefully.

JAMIE
He pulled the shed down once. When he was really – in a proper rager – but that's – as bad as it's got.

BRIONY
Were you frightened?

JAMIE
Not really. I thought it was funny. Lisa did too. Then Mum sent us upstairs. He's not like that most of the time though. Hardly ever.

BRIONY
What does your dad do when he's not working?

JAMIE
It feels like you're testing him.

BRIONY
No. I'm just trying to understand your view of him. He's – correct me if I'm wrong – a very big presence in your life and your – he was your appropriate adult.

JAMIE
Cos he doesn't judge. Cos – because he's kind. He's kind.

BRIONY
Well, that is good to know. What does he do when he's got time off?

JAMIE
Um. He likes basically all sport. My mum always says he'd watch lawn bowls and make it fun.

BRIONY
Do you watch lawn bowls with him?

JAMIE
No. Not for me.

BRIONY
You're not into sport?

JAMIE
No.

BRIONY
All of it?

JAMIE
Yeah. I'm not good at much but I'm really good at getting out of PE.

BRIONY
How did you do that?

JAMIE
Headache. Hurt my leg. Funny tummy. 'I feel a bit dizzy, sir, can I sit down for a bit.' That sort of thing.

BRIONY
And what did - does your dad make of that?

JAMIE
He didn't - doesn't know.

There's a pause. BRIONY is waiting for something.

JAMIE (CONT'D)
He knew I wasn't - sporty or anything. I used to - he used to take me to football - this football thing - Saturday mornings - and he'd stand and

cheer me on – and I'd fuck up and he'd –

BRIONY

He'd what?

Beat.

BRIONY (CONT'D)

Jamie?

Beat.

JAMIE

He'd just look away.

BRIONY

Pretend he didn't see?

JAMIE

Maybe. Or maybe – he didn't want me to see him – looking – sorry.

BRIONY

Sorry?

JAMIE

I don't know. Ashamed.

JAMIE looks at her, an exposed wound for a moment.

BRIONY

And how did you feel when you saw that? Shame?

JAMIE

You're supposed to say he wasn't.

BRIONY

Am I?

JAMIE

You're supposed to say – 'bet he wasn't ashamed – bet you just thought that, Jamie – '

BRIONY
Is that what other people have said to you?

JAMIE
'Oh, no, it wasn't what you really think - no, he wouldn't be ashamed - not of his kid' - that sort of thing.

BRIONY
You hear that a lot?

JAMIE
It's just the right thing to say.

BRIONY
Isn't it lying?

JAMIE
No. I don't know. I don't like lying.

Beat.

BRIONY
I didn't like school sport either.

JAMIE
But you were good at other stuff though, right?

BRIONY
Why do you think that?

JAMIE
You look like you were. An' you're clever so -

BRIONY
Were you not...Did you not think you were - good at anything else?

JAMIE thinks how to answer that question.

JAMIE
I didn't care I wasn't.

BRIONY meets his eyes.

BRIONY
Must be hard though to feel that way.

JAMIE
No. I think most people think like that.

BRIONY
Most people think they're bad at everything?

JAMIE
Most people are.

Beat.

BRIONY
Does your sister feel like that?

JAMIE
Lisa's clever.

BRIONY
Your dad?

JAMIE
I don't know. Mum does though.

BRIONY
Your mum thinks she's bad at everything?

JAMIE
She can cook a roast. But - yeah. I mean you'd have to ask her. But yeah.

Beat.

JAMIE (CONT'D)
I don't know. Have you - met them?

BRIONY
Your family?

JAMIE
Yeah.

BRIONY
I talked to your dad on the phone.

This half-surprises JAMIE.

JAMIE
Yeah?

BRIONY
Yes. As part of my assessment. I've also visited your school and read your reports.

JAMIE can't quite work out how to respond to that.

JAMIE
(soft)
How is he?

BRIONY
He's okay. Sad you're here. I can't say more than that.

Beat. JAMIE thinks. He tries to pull himself out of the mud.

JAMIE
Yeah.

Beat.

JAMIE (CONT'D)
Well, it's wrong. I'm here.

Beat.

JAMIE (CONT'D)
Can I ask you a question?

BRIONY
Of course you can.

JAMIE
Can you get me out of this place?

BRIONY
I'm afraid I'm of no use to you there.

JAMIE
Why couldn't they put me in a proper prison?

BRIONY
A better facility wasn't available for you.

JAMIE
But putting me in a madhouse -

BRIONY
It is a secure training centre -

JAMIE
Yeah? What they training us for? The other boys - they scream all the time.

BRIONY
I thought it had been explained -

This is tipping out of him now, his words speed up.

JAMIE
And they rock backwards and forwards, and they shout at *Coronation Street* -

BRIONY
Young offenders' institutions are for fifteen up.

JAMIE
All the way through *Corrie* –

BRIONY
You couldn't be placed in a secure school. It wasn't safe.

JAMIE
One kid goes nuts every time he sees Steve McDonald.

BRIONY
There wasn't anywhere better for you to be –

JAMIE stands up.

JAMIE
Ryan gets to stay at home till his trial –

BRIONY
Ryan wasn't accused of such a serious crime. Sit down.

JAMIE
Accused, it's all accused. If I did it, if I – hurt – her – then I'd get it – but I didn't, so...

BRIONY
As I understand it, and this wasn't my decision, this was the best place for you.

JAMIE
Will I be moved for the trial?

BRIONY
Nothing has been decided yet.

JAMIE
D'you know where it's gonna be? London or somewhere more local?

BRIONY
Honestly, Jamie, talk to Dillon, talk to anyone else, this is nothing to do with me. Back in your chair now.

JAMIE
Does that mean you don't know or you won't tell me?

BRIONY
I'm not involved in any logistics and - in terms of the progress of the case - nothing has been decided yet. You need to sit down, Jamie.

JAMIE
I don't want to sit down.

BRIONY
If you don't sit down, I have to stop this discussion -

JAMIE
Maybe I want you to...

BRIONY
Do you?

JAMIE
Piss you off that wouldn't it? You'd have to go home and then back again.

BRIONY
If you don't sit down -

He smashes what's left of his hot chocolate.

JAMIE
I DON'T WANT TO FUCKING SIT DOWN. Stop telling me to sit down all the time. You do not get to tell me what to do. Look at me now.

You do not control what I do with my life. Get that in your head.

FRANK enters the door at the side of the room.

FRANK
Everything okay? Jamie?

JAMIE
I shouted. I'm sorry.

BRIONY
There isn't a problem.

FRANK
You need him taking out for a bit?

BRIONY
No.

Beat. She's shaken, but not showing it.

BRIONY (CONT'D)
But I'll get a cup of tea. If that's okay.

JAMIE
Can I have another hot chocolate?

BRIONY
Sure.

JAMIE
You don't have to.

BRIONY
Sure.

She exits the room. FRANK watches her go.

INT. CORRIDOR. STANDLING SECURE TRAINING CENTRE

BRIONY walks down the corridor to the drinks machine.

She stands, facing it, taking some deep breaths. She's deliberately trying to calm herself down.

She hears footsteps behind her. She stiffens. She knows who it is.

VICTOR (O.S.)
Causing trouble is he?

BRIONY says nothing for a beat.

BRIONY
Can I look - into the room -

VICTOR
There's no audio.

BRIONY
Can I look -

VICTOR
Of course. Me casa is your casa.
Or whatever they say.

INT. OFFICE. STANDLING SECURE TRAINING CENTRE

VICTOR opens the door, and presses a button on the console to bring up the visitor room.

JAMIE is sitting. FRANK standing beside him. Neither is saying anything.

BRIONY opens her bag. She pulls out a notebook. She starts to read it. VICTOR tries to read it too. But she - very subtly - makes sure he can't.

VICTOR
What you seeing?

Beat. BRIONY stays intent on watching. She writes a few things down in her book. She's composing what she's going to say next.

VICTOR (CONT'D)
What you looking for? Is it body language stuff. I'm reading a book on that at the moment.

Beat.

VICTOR (CONT'D)
My sister gave it me.

Beat.

VICTOR (CONT'D)
People hide - don't need to tell you this - hide so much - but maybe they tell their truth with their bodies and their - faces.

BRIONY
Maybe.

Beat.

VICTOR
I couldn't do what you do.

BRIONY
I'm sure I couldn't do what you do.

VICTOR
You want to job swap? What are your hours? What's your pay? What's your holiday allowance?

He smiles. She writes two more things down. Then shuts the book.

BRIONY
No. I like my job. Most of the time.

VICTOR
Well, I hate mine so you're probably best off.

BRIONY
Right. That's all I needed.

VICTOR
Dib dib dib. Pleased to help.

She walks out of the room. VICTOR follows.

INT. CORRIDOR. STANDLING SECURE TRAINING CENTRE

She walks quickly down the corridor. VICTOR stands watching her, all of her, he is a creepy fucker. The camera follows her, but with eyes towards him.

As we check in with her face, BRIONY knows she's being watched.

A kid with severe tics is brought past accompanied by a large man, KEITH. She stands aside to let him go.

The kid looks accusingly towards her. She lowers her eyes, avoiding confrontation.

KEITH
Come on, Mark.

The kid follows on meekly. BRIONY watches him go. Then she turns to look at VICTOR.

Who smiles like there's nothing wrong at all.

She knocks on the door. She looks back at VICTOR, who is still smiling.

FRANK opens the door.

FRANK
Would you be more comfortable – me staying inside?

BRIONY
No. I wouldn't like that at all.

She walks into the room.

INT. VISITOR ROOM. STANDLING SECURE TRAINING CENTRE

She walks over to the table, JAMIE turns and watches her. He registers the absence of hot drinks.

She sits down. She takes a beat. She checks FRANK has shut the door.

BRIONY
Right.

She composes herself.

BRIONY (CONT'D)
I'm not a police officer, Jamie. I'm not here to elicit a confession, I'm here to understand. You think I'm trying to trick you -

JAMIE
I said that ages ago.

BRIONY
I'm not here to determine guilt or innocence, just get an understanding of your - understanding -

JAMIE half-smiles.

JAMIE
And I understand that you need to understand my understanding. Go on. Ask questions. I'll be better now.

There's a silence while she composes the right question in her head.

BRIONY
I suppose the other thing I think of when I think about masculinity is about how - masculine men feel about women.

JAMIE
We back on that?

BRIONY
Yes. Is that okay?

JAMIE
Yes. I understand you need to understand my understanding of women.

BRIONY realises.

BRIONY
I forgot your hot chocolate.

JAMIE
Doesn't matter.

BRIONY
I'll go get it -

She stands again.

JAMIE
It's fine, sit down, please. You didn't get your tea neither. It doesn't matter. I don't - didn't deserve it. I shouted. Ask your questions about women. Men. Whatever.

Beat.

BRIONY

You must have - views - on men and women - how does your dad treat your mum?

JAMIE

Are you trying to get at my dad again?

BRIONY

Not get at him.

JAMIE

Dad's actually nice to Mum.

BRIONY

You did say he tore down a shed.

JAMIE

He gets angry with himself, sometimes, but he doesn't ever hit her.

BRIONY

Does he talk to other women?

JAMIE

What?

BRIONY

Is he friendly with other women?

JAMIE

My dad? No. He loves my mum.

BRIONY

I was asking whether any of his friends were women -

JAMIE

No. His mates are his mates.

BRIONY

And they're men.

JAMIE
Is that wrong? What does that mean?

BRIONY
No. That's not wrong.

JAMIE
I thought we'd done with talking about my dad –

BRIONY
I'm just trying to –

JAMIE
Understand. I know. But none of this has anything to do with him. I'm not – to do with him.

Beat. BRIONY reconsiders her questions.

BRIONY
Fine. That's okay. Do you – Jamie – have any mates who are women?

JAMIE
No.

BRIONY
Like your dad. Your mates are – male.

JAMIE
The other shrink asks more – normal – questions – you know that?

BRIONY
Okay.

JAMIE
You want to know what he asks?

BRIONY
I can't - know.

JAMIE
I'm just saying...

BRIONY
I can't know, Jamie. My conclusions have to be independent.

JAMIE
Yeah. I won't say anything. Yeah.

Beat. BRIONY leans forward, anxious to take control again.

BRIONY
What do you think of women, Jamie?

JAMIE
I like them.

BRIONY
But you're not - like you say - particularly friends with them?

JAMIE
I'm not a twat though.

BRIONY
Are you attracted to women?

JAMIE
Yeah. I said that. I'm not gay.

BRIONY
We've established you don't have a girlfriend -

JAMIE
Yeah.

BRIONY
But I don't think I asked – before: do you want a girlfriend?

That's a stupid question.

JAMIE
Yeah. Who doesn't?

BRIONY finds her line.

BRIONY
If you had a girlfriend, what would you like to do with her?

JAMIE
What does that mean?

BRIONY
Would you like to take her out? Where would you take her?

JAMIE
I don't know. Cinema.

BRIONY
The cinema. To see what kind of film?

JAMIE
I don't know. A horror.

BRIONY
A horror film? Fifteen certificate?

JAMIE
Yeah. They're pretty slack. You can get in.

BRIONY
And after the cinema. Would you – go for a walk with her? Or take her straight home?

JAMIE
No. Not straight home.

BRIONY
Would you want to kiss her?

JAMIE
Are you allowed to ask these questions?

BRIONY
You don't discuss this in PSHE?

Beat. He smiles.

BRIONY (CONT'D)
What do you think is the normal - for your age - the normal amount someone your age would do - sexually - with a boy or a girl -

JAMIE
I told you, I'm not gay.

BRIONY
I wasn't suggesting that you were.

JAMIE
You really want me to answer?

BRIONY
If you can.

JAMIE
I don't know. Touching. Kissing.

BRIONY
What do you mean by touching?

JAMIE
Really? Touching her - bits -

BRIONY
Her chest?

JAMIE
Yeah.

BRIONY
Her backside?

JAMIE
Yeah.

BRIONY
Her vulva - her vagina?

JAMIE looks at her, incredulous.

JAMIE
I don't know. Maybe.

BRIONY
Probably not?

JAMIE
(with a shy grin)
Maybe. Are you sure you're allowed to ask these questions?

BRIONY
So you think - normal - for a thirteen-year-old boy who is heterosexual - normal for a thirteen-year-old boy to have engaged in touching of a girl's chest and her backside. Above or below clothes.

JAMIE
Below. Maybe. Above - mostly.

BRIONY smiles, reassuring him. But JAMIE misinterprets the smile. He thinks she's laughing at him. He's on edge.

JAMIE (CONT'D)
I've actually done that. So don't...Kissing and touching.

BRIONY

Okay.

JAMIE

And I've had two girls show me their tits. Sorry. Chest.

BRIONY

Okay. You don't have to use my language.

JAMIE

And I touched them. So...

BRIONY

Okay.

JAMIE

And one of them sort of touched me too, my - uh - through my trousers.

BRIONY

Okay.

JAMIE

And - I think - she liked it.

BRIONY

And you liked it?

JAMIE

Course.

Beat. He looks at her quickly. He wants to rewind.

JAMIE (CONT'D)

Not really.

BRIONY

You didn't like it?

JAMIE

I don't know.

BRIONY
There's no wrong or right answer, Jamie, in this room, you know that? Just your best attempt at the truth.

JAMIE looks down at the table.

His unhappiness seeping through. He's losing control in a different way here.

JAMIE
No. I didn't. She didn't. That didn't happen.

BRIONY
You weren't touched on your trousers?

JAMIE
Yeah. No. I wasn't.

BRIONY
And did two - girls - reveal their - go topless - with you?

Beat. He hates rewinding.

JAMIE
No. But I saw photos.

BRIONY
You saw porn photos -

JAMIE
No. Not porn. Everyone sees porn. Of two girls in my year. I saw photos. Of two girls. I knew. Know.

BRIONY notices the knew/know but doesn't make much of it.

BRIONY
You saw photos of two girls in your year topless?

JAMIE
Yeah.

BRIONY
Would they be happy you saw the photos?

JAMIE
Everyone else did.

BRIONY sits back, thinking.

BRIONY
Was Katie one of those two girls?

JAMIE looks up, shocked.

JAMIE
How d'you know that?

BRIONY
And how did it feel - to look at a picture of her?

JAMIE
How d'you guess that?

BRIONY
(because of knew/know)
I didn't guess it, I asked it. And now I want to know what it felt like - to see her - like that.

JAMIE
You asking whether I got a - ?

BRIONY
I'm asking how did it feel?

JAMIE
I liked it. Are we allowed to talk like this?

BRIONY
How does it make you feel looking at naked pictures of women?

JAMIE
How d'you think?

BRIONY
In particular, how would you describe the way you feel looking at naked pictures of people you know?

JAMIE
I don't know. Good.

BRIONY
Does it make you feel powerful? Do you feel like it gives you a power?

JAMIE
No. That's weird.

Beat.

BRIONY
Were you attracted to Katie?

JAMIE
She wasn't my type.

BRIONY
So you weren't?

JAMIE
She was quite - no offence - quite flat, you know?

BRIONY
Right.

JAMIE

Everyone said it. Who saw it. That's not just me. Picture got passed around the school. Snapchat you know. And it was just her - top half. Not - not anything else. She sent it to Fidget - and he sent it on.

BRIONY

Why did she send it to Fidget?

JAMIE

I don't know. She fancied him?

BRIONY

She was trying to attract him?

JAMIE

And I think he asked her. Not going to get any more pictures though, is he?

BRIONY

No. She's dead.

JAMIE looks at her, stung.

JAMIE

No. I didn't mean from her. I meant - from other girls. No one'll send him other pictures because he wasn't careful with the one he got. The twat.

BRIONY

You think he should have collected more pictures from more girls before he shared them with other boys?

JAMIE

Yeah? I don't know.

Beat.

JAMIE (CONT'D)
Why d'you say 'she's dead' like that?

BRIONY
Because she is.

Beat. We see BRIONY question herself for a moment as JAMIE looks at her carefully.

She wants to place every step she takes securely.

She knows exactly what understanding she needs to reach.

BRIONY (CONT'D)
Do you think - Jamie - I've asked you if you're attracted to women - do you think women are attracted to you?

JAMIE
What sort of question is that?

BRIONY
What do you think? Do you think - girls - are attracted to you?

JAMIE
No. Of course not.

BRIONY
Why of course not?

How the fuck is he supposed to answer this? He tries truth.

JAMIE
Because I'm - ugly.

BRIONY
And how does that make you feel?

He hates this.

JAMIE

Aren't you supposed to say I'm not ugly?

BRIONY

What I think isn't important –

JAMIE

Yeah, you don't say stuff that normal people say –

BRIONY

How would it make you feel if I did say 'you're not ugly'?

JAMIE

I just – don't know why you don't say the things normal people say.

BRIONY

You thought I should have contradicted you when you said your dad was ashamed of you – and you think I should contradict you now when you tell me you think yourself ugly.

JAMIE

I don't know.

Beat. She keeps her eyes down.

BRIONY

What I'm interested in is the fact you think you're ugly, Jamie.

JAMIE

(with a hurt smile)

Yeah. I'm fascinating.

BRIONY

I'm interested in it because what you think is more important to me than what is true, okay? So - how do you feel about being ugly.

JAMIE starts to get worked up.

JAMIE
How would you feel? You don't know. You're not. You're dead pretty.

BRIONY
This is not about me, Jamie.

JAMIE
You don't think you're pretty?

BRIONY
I am not the interesting person in this room.

JAMIE
You don't think you're pretty - you do think I'm ugly.

BRIONY
I haven't passed judgement on either of those things. If you think about it - for very good reason.

JAMIE
'For very good reason.'

BRIONY
I want to understand you.

JAMIE is getting seriously worked up.

JAMIE
To understand my understanding of my understanding of my understanding -

BRIONY
Yes.

JAMIE
The other bloke is much more easy. Him, checking whether I understand was much easier -

BRIONY
They need two opinions for a reason. This is how I like to establish my assessment.

JAMIE
Whether I understand what I did -

He thumps the table, looking at the cameras in the room.

JAMIE (CONT'D)
I didn't say that so don't go - thinking that I did - I was just getting mixed up because she was making me -

He stands up.

BRIONY, her adrenalin rising, looks down at her extremely conservative clothes. She keeps herself under control. She doesn't look at JAMIE.

He walks around the room.

FRANK enters the room, BRIONY signals with her hand for him to leave, he does. JAMIE notices.

JAMIE (CONT'D)
What was that? What was that? What the fuck? Signalling him away like a fucking - queen?

He gets right in her face, staring.

BRIONY
You want to come and sit back down, Jamie?

JAMIE
Fuck off. Fucking bitch.

BRIONY
(firm)
Jamie, I need you to sit down.

JAMIE looks at her for a long moment.

JAMIE
Rah!

BRIONY jumps, but tries to hide it.

She doesn't want him breaking the power dynamics of the room.

He takes a breath. He wants to scream. He doesn't scream.

He takes another breath. He controls himself.

He shoves at his chair.

He walks around the room, calming down.

BRIONY
Are you going to sit down?

JAMIE
Fuck off!

He continues pacing. She waits in silence. Eventually, he picks up his chair and comes to sit back down.

JAMIE (CONT'D)
Go on then, go. Are you going?

BRIONY
Would you like me to?

JAMIE
It's not up to me, is it?

BRIONY
If you want me to go, Jamie,
I can go.

Beat.

BRIONY (CONT'D)
You said in our previous sessions that you had friends - Ryan and Tommy, but that you weren't - popular -

JAMIE
Yes.

BRIONY
You said you would consider yourself bullied. The three of you were bullied.

JAMIE
People like you love talking about bullying.

BRIONY
You said Tommy was called Round Pounds because his mum bought her shopping from Poundland.

JAMIE
Yeah. She doesn't -

BRIONY
And that Ryan was called dumb -

JAMIE
Ryan is dumb. That one was sort of true -

BRIONY
You said that the three of you felt ostracised quite a lot.

JAMIE
Big words coming out now.

BRIONY
You said sometimes this got physical. That sometimes people would spit on your back from the windows of classrooms. How you'd be tripped up a lot. Pushed.

JAMIE
Yeah.

BRIONY
You were called names and you were physically abused...

JAMIE
Just tripped and spat on.

BRIONY
My question is then, Jamie, why do you have an Instagram account?

JAMIE
What? Need one.

BRIONY
Why?

JAMIE
To look at other people's Instagram accounts. You can't if you haven't got one.

BRIONY
Right. You follow lots of women on Instagram. Models.

JAMIE
Yeah.

BRIONY
You don't need to put photos up though. Why do you put photos up? Of yourself I mean...

This feels more difficult.

JAMIE
I don't know.

BRIONY
To show - the fun you have with Tommy and Ryan? To prove those bullies wrong?

JAMIE
No.

BRIONY
To show the fun you have with your family?

JAMIE
No way am I putting anything up of them. You seen anything like that it's cos my sister tagged me -

BRIONY
Because you think someone might like one of your photos - you might get into a conversation? Make a new friend - meet a girl -

JAMIE
(yes)
No.

BRIONY takes a breath. She knows she's getting to the nub of this.

BRIONY
Katie commented on your photos on a number of different occasions...

JAMIE
Yeah.

BRIONY
She wrote this -

She stands to get her bag from near the table.

JAMIE
What are you doing? Are you allowed to ask this stuff? Has Dillon passed these questions fit?

BRIONY
I am allowed to ask about intimacies. If it makes you uncomfortable, or makes you ask questions, there are other people in this facility who can help you with that.

JAMIE
I'm fine with girls.

Beat. BRIONY takes some printouts from her bag.

BRIONY
Katie wrote this on your Facebook feed -

JAMIE
(Jesus Christ)
Facebook??

BRIONY
Instagram -

JAMIE
Are you okay? You look a bit red? Did I scare you when I shouted?

BRIONY
She wrote this on your Instagram feed -

JAMIE
Because I'm only thirteen and don't think I look that - scary so -

BRIONY
What do these emojis mean?

JAMIE
How embarrassing is that? Wow.

BRIONY
Can you tell me what these emojis mean? What does the kidney beans mean? These are kidney beans, right?

JAMIE thinks - does he want to tell her this?

JAMIE
She's pretending like I'm part of one of those truth groups -

BRIONY
What truth groups?

JAMIE
Ones that say women don't want us and we don't care -

BRIONY
Are you? Part of those?

JAMIE
No.

BRIONY
But you know what they say.

JAMIE
Because - everyone kept going on about it. Incel stuff. So I had a look. I didn't really like it.

BRIONY
And was that - was you being an incel - was that what she was saying with all of these?

She lays copies of all the emojis on the table. There's the red kidney beans, the dynamite and the '100%', and a bow-wrapped heart.

JAMIE
Yeah.

BRIONY
Can you explain them all?

JAMIE sits back, looks at her, thinks and then points to the heart.

JAMIE
Want love. Won't get it.

Points to the dynamite.

JAMIE (CONT'D)
Red pill exploding. Same thing as red pill. And then this is an eighty-twenty thing.

BRIONY
What's an eighty-twenty thing?

JAMIE
Eighty per cent of women are attracted to twenty per cent of men. I think they're probably right about that bit. I mean that's just - right.

He sits in that for a moment. BRIONY looks at him carefully.

BRIONY
And people liked her comments - quite a lot -

JAMIE
Yeah. They thought it was funny.

BRIONY
You must have found that quite cruel?

JAMIE
Yeah. I s'pose.

BRIONY
Did she do this to other people too?

JAMIE
No.

BRIONY
Why did she do it to you?

JAMIE
Cos I'm ugly. Wah-wah.

BRIONY
You think that's why she did it to you?

JAMIE
I'm the ugliest I suppose so –

BRIONY
Did you call her on it?

JAMIE
Yeah.

BRIONY
What did you say?

JAMIE
I don't know. I'm not what you say I am or...

BRIONY
And what did she say?

JAMIE
She said 'okay' and then smiled and walked away.

BRIONY
Did you never think to tell anyone else what she was doing?

JAMIE
Bit late for that now isn't it?

Beat. BRIONY digests this.

BRIONY
All this. That must have hurt.

JAMIE
I didn't kill her.

BRIONY thinks then JAMIE takes an unerring step forward.

JAMIE (CONT'D)
You think I did because you've seen the video. But you can't trust video no more. Fake news. Fake news.

BRIONY
I'm not here to judge -

JAMIE
I didn't kill her. She was a bitch. You can see that. I should have killed her. But I didn't. All I did -

BRIONY waits.

JAMIE (CONT'D)
All I did -

BRIONY waits again. JAMIE laughs.

JAMIE (CONT'D)
Look at you. All hopeful. Like I'm going to say something important.

BRIONY smiles. But it's a real mask now.

JAMIE (CONT'D)
All I did. I did ask her out. After the photo. I went round and said I was sorry and that - that Fidget had done that - shown everyone her ti(ts) - chest - and I wanted to know if she'd come up the fair - with me.

There's a silence. BRIONY wants him to continue, but knows not to prompt.

JAMIE (CONT'D)
I just thought she might be - weak. At that - I thought she might be - weak. So I just thought I'd ask her - if she wanted to go to the fair - because everyone else was calling her a slag you know - or flat - or - so I thought when she was like that - weak - she might - like me.

He looks up at BRIONY. His need and insecurity flooding out of him.

JAMIE (CONT'D)
Clever don't you think?

BRIONY
To ask her out when everyone else didn't like her?

JAMIE
I told her I was sorry they'd done that to her, that Fidget was a wanker, and then I said I'd take her to the fair if she liked.

Beat. He's reliving it.

BRIONY

Her weakness - made her more gettable - that was your theory?

JAMIE

Yeah.

BRIONY

I thought you said you didn't find her attractive?

JAMIE

She is flat. That's fact. But that's okay. I didn't mind that. I wore my best tracksuit. I don't know why I'm telling you this. And I said - you want to come up the fair?

BRIONY

And what did she say?

And this is the worst bit of all for him.

JAMIE

She, uh...Just - laughed. Said she wasn't that desperate.

Beat. He relives that too.

BRIONY

Right.

BRIONY is trying to work out how to navigate this situation.

BRIONY (CONT'D)

And the emoji messages came after that?

JAMIE

Yeah.

BRIONY
She was – let's say – attacking you for presuming you could ask her out?

JAMIE
Your words.

BRIONY
You think they're unfair?

JAMIE
You think she was a bitch, right? Doing that? You think she was a bullying bitch? She was a bullying bitch, right?

Beat. He's really worked up now.

JAMIE (CONT'D)
But there's – that's – the thing, you see – I didn't even – that night – I didn't touch her – I *could* have touched her – I didn't touch her – I had a knife, she was scared, I could have touched any part of her body I wanted to – I really wanted to – but I didn't – I just –

Beat.

JAMIE (CONT'D)
Most boys would have touched her. So that makes me better.

Beat. BRIONY can't look at him for a moment.

JAMIE (CONT'D)
That makes me better, don't you think?

BRIONY says nothing.

There's a long silence.

JAMIE picks up and forlornly takes a bite of the sandwich.

BRIONY looks up and watches him do so.

He coughs, on a crumb. He coughs repeatedly.

And then he spits it out, with it a piece of sandwich falls onto the floor.

And then he sits back. We see him piece together everything he just said. Relive it.

JAMIE (CONT'D)
No. I didn't mean that. I'm just tired.

Beat.

JAMIE (CONT'D)
I'm talking too much and I'm tired.

Beat.

JAMIE (CONT'D)
I didn't kill her.

BRIONY
Jamie, do you understand what death is?

JAMIE
What?

BRIONY
Do you understand what death is?

JAMIE
Yeah.

BRIONY
Do you understand that Katie is gone and she can't come back?

JAMIE
I didn't kill her.

BRIONY
That whatever claims you make as to her character –

JAMIE
I didn't mean she was a bitch.

BRIONY
That whatever claims you make about her, she is gone. That whoever did kill her – that they extinguished the possibility of her future life?

JAMIE
I didn't mean to be mean about her. She wasn't so bad. She just didn't like me. She wasn't so bad otherwise.

BRIONY
Do you understand?

JAMIE
Yeah.

BRIONY
Do you understand that murder is a crime?

JAMIE
I didn't do it.

BRIONY
Do you understand it?

JAMIE
Yeah.

BRIONY
Do you understand if you are found guilty of that crime you will be held in detention.

JAMIE
Who doesn't know that?

BRIONY
Do you understand who'll make the decision about that?

JAMIE
Judge. Jury.

BRIONY
Okay.

She takes a beat.

BRIONY (CONT'D)
Okay. Jamie, this is our last session -

JAMIE
What? Why?

BRIONY
But what I'd encourage you to do - whatever happens next - is take advantage of any mental health services you're offered -

JAMIE
Why?

BRIONY
I think you will benefit from talking more about all these things -

JAMIE
No.

BRIONY
That's what I think.

JAMIE
Then you come back. You see me.

BRIONY
Unfortunately I'm needed elsewhere.

JAMIE looks up at her, trying to work this out.

JAMIE
I can't believe this is just it. Like, fucking, done.

BRIONY
I do hope you take what I said seriously. Thanks for your time. I'll ask Frank to come back in now.

JAMIE
Thanks for my time?

BRIONY
And honesty. I'm grateful you talked to me as honestly as you did.

BRIONY looks up at the camera and makes a 'come in' signal.

JAMIE
You think I'm honest? Will you tell the judge?

BRIONY
I think you've spoken to me with honesty but all I'm advising the judge on is –

JAMIE
My understanding.

BRIONY

Yes.

Beat.

JAMIE

Doesn't seem like a proper goodbye.

BRIONY

It is.

JAMIE

Doesn't seem like one.

FRANK enters the room. JAMIE looks at him, panicked.

JAMIE (CONT'D)

We haven't finished.

BRIONY

We have. Thanks Frank.

JAMIE

No.

Beat. JAMIE doesn't want her to go.

JAMIE (CONT'D)

No. No. Can I ask you something?

BRIONY

Of course you can.

JAMIE

Do you like me?

Beat. She's really surprised by that question. He's really surprised to have asked it.

There's a silence. He reads her face. His face falls.

JAMIE (CONT'D)

Oh. You don't.

BRIONY
My job was to assess you, Jamie -

JAMIE
Don't you think like that then?

BRIONY
I was just here to assess you as a professional -

JAMIE
Because I like you. Not like that. Not fancying you. Not really. Just as a person.

FRANK
Okay, son, come on now.

JAMIE
Don't you even like me a bit?

BRIONY looks at him.

JAMIE (CONT'D)
What did you think? About me then? Decide?

BRIONY
This was really useful.

JAMIE
I didn't do it so don't go telling people - don't you dare.

Beat.

FRANK
Come on, Jamie. I like you enough for everyone. Come on. Let's take you back to your room.

JAMIE is led from the room. He calls back.

JAMIE
Don't you even like me a bit? What did you think about me then?

Tell my dad I'm okay. Tell my dad I'm okay. TELL MY DAD I'M OKAY.

BRIONY is left.

She stays stock-still, trying to control her environment.

The room is spinning but she's not letting it.

She folds the cling film the sandwich was in.

She folds it carefully into a small piece.

She puts it in her bag.

Then she takes it out of her bag and puts it in the empty hot chocolate cup.

She doesn't want a trace of him with her.

She gets up slowly. She looks around, she wobbles just a tiny bit.

She takes a breath.

CREDITS.

EPISODE FOUR

Christine Tremarco (as Manda Miller) and Stephen Graham (as Eddie Miller), courtesy of Netflix © 2024

THIRTEEN MONTHS

EXT. GARDEN. MILLER HOUSE

The camera is in the garden shed with the door open, as we see EDDIE enter, putting away the lawnmower. Busying himself.

In doing so, he spots Jamie's BMX bike with MAG WHEELS, rusting in the shed.

He stops.

He puts on a game face.

He closes the door and walks across the garden. He picks up his coffee cup and takes a drink before heading into the -

INT. LIVING ROOM/KITCHEN. MILLER HOUSE

Living room and then into the kitchen, where MANDA is slicing black pudding. EDDIE smiles.

EDDIE
That smells lovely that.

MANDA
Well it is your birthday. I don't mind cooking you a full English once a year.

She kisses him. He smiles.

MANDA (CONT'D)
Happy birthday, old man.
I married an old man.

EDDIE
You're getting younger are you?

MANDA
I am you cheeky git. I've taken a special pill.

He looks at what she's doing.

EDDIE
What's that, black pudding?

She laughs, she knew this would excite him.

MANDA
It's from the butcher 'n' all.

EDDIE
(with a grin)
It's very bad for me.

MANDA
I know. But you like it very much.

EDDIE
I like you more.

MANDA
But only when I'm doing you a fry-up.

He puts his hands around her waist.

EDDIE
No. Not only then. Especially at Christmas when you've got your suzzies on.

He reaches his hand upwards.

MANDA
Oi. You leave my suspenders out of it. Later!

EDDIE
I'll only be five minutes.

MANDA
You're never five minutes!

EDDIE
Lisa will be asleep till twelve.

MANDA
She won't sleep till twelve on her dad's fiftieth.

He kisses her. His hands travel north again.

MANDA (CONT'D)
Come on. Cards! Concentrate on birthday cards.

EDDIE
You're such a spoilsport.

EDDIE sits down at the table.

MANDA
Eggs? Scrambled or poached?

EDDIE
Fried.

MANDA
You're dying young.

EDDIE
I'm dying happy.

She laughs and EDDIE riffles through the cards. He opens a card.

EDDIE (CONT'D)
From me dad and Jean. Written by Jean. With a fiver. Can't even buy a pint for a fiver these days.

He puts it down and picks up another.

His face falls, he opens it.

It's a hand-drawn picture of his face. It's good. It's not exceptional, but it's good.

It says 'Happy Birthday' at the top in bubble writing.

He looks at it for a long time.

He opens the card.

It simply says 'Love J' inside.

EDDIE nods to himself.

MANDA
Who's that from?

He shows her, holding it up as she walks over.

MANDA (CONT'D)
It's a lovely picture. He's almost made you look handsome.

She smiles, hoping he'll smile too. He doesn't. He takes in the card once more.

EDDIE
It's good innit.

MANDA
He's put the effort in.

EDDIE
Yeah.

LISA flies down the stairs and to the front door, opening it.

LISA
SHIT! DAD! Can you come outside please?!

EDDIE
Lisa? What's going on?

EDDIE doesn't look at MANDA as he follows his daughter out.

EXT. MILLER HOUSE

EDDIE leaves the house, to see what has been sprayed down the side of his work van, a van with Miller Plumbing written on it: the word 'NONSE'.

We look at it a beat.

EDDIE takes a beat.

MANDA comes out of the house.

He touches the paint. He examines it on his fingers.

LISA
Sorry Dad. Sorry.

EDDIE stares at the van.

EDDIE
It's not your fault.

LISA
They're such dickheads.

EDDIE
Oi, language.

LISA
Sorry.

EDDIE notices EILEEN across the road watching beadily.

He points at the van.

EDDIE
Did you see anything, Eileen?

EILEEN
No, nothing.

EDDIE
You didn't see a thing, no?

EILEEN
Sorry. It's been quiet this morning.

EDDIE turns to MANDA.

EDDIE
Call the police.

MANDA
Again you think?

EDDIE
He said to call them if anything else happens.

MANDA goes inside.

LISA
I'm sorry, Dad. Happy birthday.

EDDIE
It's alright, love.

He looks back at the van.

He notices FRANKY come out of a house further down.

EDDIE (CONT'D)
(not as quiet but still quiet)
Ah look. They're all coming out now.

He raises a hand.

EDDIE (CONT'D)
Morning mate. Don't suppose you seen anything, did you? Ey? Bet none of you did.

FRANKY doesn't say anything back, but does raise a hand. EDDIE looks at his daughter.

EDDIE (CONT'D)
Bit of soap and water, I'll get this off.

He throws a look at EILEEN as he heads back towards the front door.

EDDIE (CONT'D)
Can't believe you didn't see anything!

EDDIE enters back into the house.

The camera lingers with LISA looking at the side of the van. She feels FRANKY still staring, and turns back inside.

INT. HALLWAY. MILLER HOUSE

MANDA is stood talking on her phone.

We catch up with her as EDDIE walks past her into the kitchen.

PHONE
(So when did this happen?)

MANDA
Overnight...

PHONE
(Do you know what time it happened?)

MANDA
No, we don't know when...When was the last time you saw the van, love?

EDDIE
What?

EDDIE turns back towards MANDA.

MANDA
Last night. When was the last time you saw the van?

EDDIE
I've no idea. What time did I get back?

MANDA
What time did you park up?

EDDIE remembers something.

EDDIE
About eight o'clock when I parked up.

MANDA
Eight p.m. till now...

PHONE
(What have they written? What does it say?)

MANDA
Nonce...

PHONE
(And how have they spelt it?)

MANDA
N - o - n - s - e...

PHONE
(It should be with a C.)

MANDA
Yeah, I can see that...

PHONE
(Do you know who it's directed to?)

MANDA
I don't know, is that for me to decide? Maybe they think Jamie's a nonce, maybe they think Eddie is one...

PHONE
(Okay Mrs Miller.)

EDDIE stiffens.

MANDA
Shall I take a picture?

PHONE
(We'll need to come out, so please don't touch it until we do.)

MANDA
No, me husband's taking it off...

PHONE
(Could you wait for the police to arrive?)

MANDA
No, we're not waiting, I'll take a picture...

PHONE
(We'll still need to document the crime ourselves in person.)

MANDA
I'll tell you what, I'll take three pictures for you then. And I'll get my daughter to email it to you, love.

MANDA passes the phone to LISA.

MANDA (CONT'D)
Email the photos to Sam.

INT. KITCHEN. MILLER HOUSE

MANDA enters and the camera follows her.

We see EDDIE turn on the tap and pour washing-up liquid into a bucket.

She's furious and is now able to show it.

MANDA
Little twats.

EDDIE
Just calm down, love.

MANDA
It's your birthday.

He searches under the sink for sponges and cloths, he finds some.

EDDIE
They weren't to know that, just please stay calm for our Lisa.

Beat.

MANDA
(dangerous)
Thanks for letting me know what I should be doing...

EDDIE
I'm not telling you what you should be doing, I'm just saying - think about our Lisa.

Beat.

MANDA
I've had enough of this, Eddie.

EDDIE turns back to her from the sink.

EDDIE
Look, love, before you say anything...

MANDA
What am I saying?

EDDIE
You know what you're saying. We're not doing this. We've been through this, we're not going down this road again and we're not moving.

MANDA
He's in the dock in four weeks and then everyone will be having a stare.

EDDIE
But not at us. And he's behind a screen. They're hiding him.

MANDA
Yeah, and they're doing a great job of hiding him.

EDDIE
And they're protecting him. We've been through all this, love.

EDDIE turns back to filling the bucket.

MANDA
This isn't going to get any better.

He ignores her.

MANDA (CONT'D)
My mum says she can get you work.

He turns, exploding.

EDDIE
I don't need your mum to get me work! Why would I want your mum to get me work! I've got work here. I've got clients, loyal clients. I've got jobs here. I've got lads that depend on me. Lisa's got college. Do you want

to take her out? You've got your job. You love that job and you won't get a better job than that anywhere else. And Liverpool? You think Liverpool will be any better, cos I'm telling you now, it'll be ten times worse and you know that. We've done nothing wrong, love, have we? Have we done anything wrong?

MANDA

No.

EDDIE

No. So we're not moving, Mand.

He goes back to the sink for the bucket, he picks it up too roughly and it sloshes all over his trousers and the floor.

EDDIE (CONT'D)

Sorry. Sorry about that. Don't worry, love, I'll clean that up. Sorry.

MANDA gets a cloth and quickly dries the floor.

We continue out with EDDIE.

Past LISA, who is sat on the stairs.

LISA

Dad.

EDDIE

What are you doing there? You shouldn't be listening. Don't worry, love, I'll get this off.

EDDIE exits with his bucket of water as we continue up the stairs with LISA.

INT. STAIRS. MILLER HOUSE

LISA passes the room we know as Jamie's room but she doesn't stop.

We follow her into -

INT. LISA'S ROOM. MILLER HOUSE

Her own room.

Where LISA picks up her phone and texts someone. MANDA comes in.

MANDA
Did you send the email?

LISA
Jesus Christ, don't you knock anymore?

MANDA
Did you send it?

LISA
Yes I did.

MANDA
Who you texting?

LISA
Billy.

MANDA
Oh. Right. How is that?

LISA
None of yours.

There's a silence.

LISA (CONT'D)
Is Dad...?

MANDA
I'm giving him space. Cos that's what I do.

LISA
He loves that van.

MANDA
He depends on that van. He doesn't love it. It'll be okay.

LISA
You really think soap and water will do anything?

MANDA
I don't know anything about paint, do you?

LISA
You're furious.

MANDA
I'm not.

LISA doesn't know whether to poke further.

LISA
Who's supposed to be the nonce anyway? Jamie's thirteen years old and it's obviously not Dad, the fucking idiots they probably don't even know what it means...

A beat.

LISA (CONT'D)
And Jamie wasn't that...

The word 'Jamie' has an electricity. MANDA looks at her daughter, unsure quite how to phrase what comes next.

MANDA
Found myself in his room the other day. Giving it a hoover.

LISA
Yeah?

MANDA
Didn't know what to do really -

LISA
I don't go in.

MANDA nods.

MANDA
But you're okay - Billy's looking after you -

LISA
Billy's not looking after me, Mum. Can you please stop saying that? I look after me, alright?

MANDA sways slightly.

LISA (CONT'D)
And no one's written nonce on my locker. So there's that.

EDDIE shouts up the stairs.

EDDIE (O.S.)
Manda, where's that big scrubbing brush?

MANDA
Under the sink.

EDDIE (O.S.)
It's not there.

MANDA
Check under the sink. Keep looking.

EDDIE (O.S.)
I am looking!

MANDA
I'll go and help your dad. Do you want a cup of tea.

LISA
No.

MANDA
Okay. Love you...

LISA doesn't respond. MANDA exits for the stairs.

MANDA (CONT'D)
I love you too.

LISA looks after her.

The camera follows MANDA.

INT. STAIRS. MILLER HOUSE

She walks down the stairs.

Her face tired. Her whole body tired. EDDIE passes her with the scrubbing brush.

MANDA
Do you want a cup of tea?

EDDIE
No you're okay.

EXT. MILLER HOUSE

EDDIE starts scrubbing at the van's paintwork.

Some is coming off. Not much is coming off.

He scrubs again. Going really hard. His face reddening as he puts in maximum effort.

He sees a curtain twitch from opposite.

EDDIE
Alright Eileen? Need a chair bringing and a nice cup of tea? Bit of birthday cake?

He gets back to work with the soap and water, as kids on bikes ride past. We recognise one of them as FREDO (from Episode Two), the other is a lad called PAUL.

FREDO
(laughing)
Nonce.

EDDIE, hearing this, charges after them.

EDDIE
What? What did you say?

FREDO rides on really fast.

EDDIE (CONT'D)
Ey! Oi! Oi!

He shouts after them.

EDDIE (CONT'D)
Did you do that to my van?

The boys ride on.

He stands a moment more. His anger pulsing. He looks back at the van. He begins to scrub again. It's not budging.

Then he dumps the sponge back into the bucket and picks it up, carrying it back in.

INT. KITCHEN / HALLWAY. MILLER HOUSE

He comes through the kitchen and pours the water away.

EDDIE
It's not coming off.

MANDA
Do you want to try some bleach?

EDDIE
That won't work. We'll have to go to Wainwrights.

MANDA
What, now?

EDDIE
Yeah, now, we'll have to go to Wainwrights now.

MANDA
Why?

EDDIE
Because I need to get it off! I can't turn up for work with that on my van.

MANDA
I know but -

EDDIE
So come on, let's go now, we won't be long. LISA, GRAB YOUR JACKET LOVE.

LISA (O.S.)
What?

INT. HALLWAY. MILLER HOUSE

They go through into the hall, EDDIE hands MANDA her jacket as LISA appears at the top of the stairs.

EDDIE
Put your coat on, we're going to Wainwrights.

LISA
Can't I just stay here?

EDDIE
We've just had someone vandalise our van, who knows what's next.

LISA
Why would I want to go?

EDDIE
Because I'm asking you to go.

MANDA
Eddie, I've got breakfast on.

EDDIE
Girls please! Please, do me a favour. Help me out, please, I'm trying.

EDDIE looks up at MANDA, she can see the effort on his face. She melts seamlessly in with him. She's good at that.

MANDA
No you're right, we'll all go. Get the day back.

EDDIE
(grateful)
That's it. Let's get the day back, eh? For my birthday.

LISA
And going to Wainwrights is
a birthday treat?

MANDA laughs.

EDDIE
It is for me. I used to have
fuck-all when I was a kid, count
yourself lucky.

EXT. MILLER HOUSE / INT. VAN

He opens the van with his keys and ushers them out before locking the door behind himself and following the girls to the van.

EDDIE
Keep an eye on our house, Eileen
love, would you?

EILEEN (O.S.)
Course I will.

EDDIE gets in.

EDDIE
(under his breath)
Don't forget to text the
Neighbourhood Watch as well.

LISA looks at her mum as she gets in. They all fit together on the wide front seat.

EDDIE puts his hands on the steering wheel.

We study his face. It's determined. Almost manic, but not quite. He's trying desperately to find the joy.

EDDIE (CONT'D)
Right. Belts on. New day. New
start. Tunes. Lisa, pick one.

Only rule, has to involve a bass line.

LISA

What?

He starts the van.

EDDIE

All good music has to have a bass line.

LISA

(to MANDA)

What's he on about?

MANDA smiles and encourages LISA to go with it. EDDIE notices this.

EDDIE

I have worked out that all good music involves a bass guitar. None of this plinky-plonky shit and drum and bass bollocks. Give me a bass line I can nip my teeth in.

MANDA

You talk such rubbish.

EDDIE laughs. He drives away.

EDDIE

Which brings me onto another thing, after we've been to Wainwrights and I've got this off the van, I want us to go on - an outing.

MANDA

An outing?

EDDIE

A family outing.

MANDA laughs at this new mood of EDDIE's.

MANDA
And what will you do on your family outing?

EDDIE
To a - I don't know. Go up a hill.

MANDA
A hill?!

EDDIE
Or a zoo.

MANDA laughs.

LISA
I'm not going to a bloody zoo. I'm nearly eighteen.

EDDIE
Or a - ice-skating.

MANDA
You - ice-skating?

EDDIE
What's wrong with me ice-skating? Alright, the pictures.

LISA
(quickly)
I'd do that.

EDDIE
The pictures?

LISA
If I have to do something.

EDDIE
That's good. Manda, look what's on on the tinterweb.

MANDA
I'm looking at you. What's into you?

EDDIE
(warning)
I'm just interested in solving the problem of today, okay?

MANDA
(warning)
And I'm helping -

She's pulling him back from his slightly manic place. He looks at her, he nods.

LISA leans forward.

LISA
Sorry. Solving the problem of today?

MANDA
He's doing a...That's what the - therapist has -

LISA
What we solving?

EDDIE
Nothing. I just think the pictures is a great idea.

MANDA
We'll have breakfast first though eh?

EDDIE
Yes. Wainwrights. Me and our Lisa will take the paint off when we get back, while you cook the breakfast.

MANDA
That sounds - yeah.

They smile in complicity. MANDA looks in her phone. She starts scrolling through.

EDDIE
Then breakfast. Lovely black pudding.

LISA
Lovely black pudding?

MANDA
I got it in for your dad.

LISA
(to her dad)
You're dying young.

MANDA
I said that.

EDDIE
And I'm having fried bread.

MANDA
I got some nice bread in for that too.

EDDIE
Your mother is a *fine* woman.

LISA
So you tell me.

MANDA
Oi!

They're laughing.

EDDIE
Then we'll go to the pictures. And we'll have a big tub of popcorn for our lunch. Then back home and –

LISA
Can we get Chinese for tea.

EDDIE
(delighted)
Yes we can!

He thumps the steering wheel.

EDDIE (CONT'D)
This is good. We've got our day back, kids.

LISA
It's been ages since I've gone to the cinema.

EDDIE
What's the tune?

LISA
I can't think of any that have got bass – I don't really know which have got bass –

MANDA
'Take On Me'. A-ha.

EDDIE laughs. MANDA smiles. Things are genuinely beginning to grow now.

LISA
What?

MANDA
Your dad –

EDDIE
(still laughing)
No, no, I don't know they had a bass player, Manda, actually.

MANDA
Pal. Paul. He played bass, the keyboard, everything...

EDDIE
I forgot you were in the fan club. Your ma had posters on her walls, badges, scarves, the works.

LISA
I don't get it.

MANDA
Your dad. One school disco. When we were – we were just going out –

EDDIE
You ever think we've been together too long?

MANDA
Just going out. Early days. And you decided to test me...

EDDIE smiles.

EDDIE
No. No. No testing. It wasn't a test –

MANDA
He wore this daft pink wig. And everyone was laughing, but your dad never cared when people laughed at him...

EDDIE
Hang about – didn't I?

MANDA
And it was the beginning of the night and so no one was dancing yet because they never did – we were what, thirteen?

EDDIE
Yeah. Third year.

MANDA
(to LISA)
That's Year Nine in your language.

She turns back to EDDIE.

MANDA (CONT'D)
And the DJ - Mr Barnes the geography teacher - was getting desperate, and A-ha is a pretty good floor-filler - but still no one got dancing, the whole hall was empty with - shyness - and your dad - your dad - this was bonkers - just started dancing - on his own - middle of the floor -

EDDIE
Mr Barnes needed the help -

MANDA
And everyone just - laughed and watched -

LISA
Dad!

EDDIE
I was actually a pretty good mover. They were probably enjoying my audacious steps.

MANDA
And then - oh my -

She's really laughing.

EDDIE
Easy. You'll hurt yourself laughing like that.

LISA
What?

MANDA
About halfway through, he was slipping and sliding all over the floor –

EDDIE
I'd found a pair of bowling shoes in a charity shop to go with the wig.

LISA
What? Dad!

EDDIE
White-and-red striped.

MANDA
And he slipped too far – slid and split his legs in two and landed flat on his face –

LISA is laughing. They're all laughing.

EDDIE
Those shoes were a hazard. Dancing in them seems alright when you've scored a strike, but they're not made for special moves.

MANDA
And he stood up, and he'd banged his nose and there was blood hammering down his face and everyone was just pissing themselves, and he said – 'I'm bleeding here.'

LISA laughs.

EDDIE
'I'm bleeding here.'

MANDA
For years at school after that - it just became - people would just say it - 'I'm bleeding here!'

EDDIE grins.

MANDA presses play on her phone. 'Take On Me' comes through the van speakers.

EDDIE smiles bigger.

EDDIE
I wish I'd kept those bowling shoes. Those bowling shoes were something special.

LISA
(dry)
They sound it.

He sings along. MANDA joins in.

EDDIE
I only know bits, your mum was mad on 'em.

LISA
This is - awful.

MANDA
You proud? You're proud, aren't you.

LISA looks out of the window, shrinking from her parents and desperate no one sees.

EDDIE
Here it comes...

Together they pound out the chorus.

LISA
If anyone sees - I'm getting out of this van even if it's moving...

But she's laughing.

MANDA
I loved them all. I'd have done anything for any of them.

EDDIE
She means that, too. You could have looked quite different, my girl.

LISA
When did you fall over? Will you tell me exactly when?

MANDA
End of the second verse...
It's here. It's now...

They both shout together.

EDDIE
I'M BLEEDING HERE!

MANDA
I'M BLEEDING HERE!

EDDIE
You're terrible!

They all really laugh. And then LISA registers what they just said, and we see it play across her face.

The tune continues to go. She looks at her mum and dad, neither of whom have realised.

MANDA
Rest of the night, we just stayed sat together didn't we?

EDDIE
Weren't going to dance again was I? Those bowling shoes had no grip.

They park up in Wainwrights.

There's a silence.

MANDA
And then you walked me home - I walked, you slid - and my parents were waiting up and my dad asked you if you'd been in a fight, and you said 'something like that'.

EDDIE
And then you snogged my face off.

LISA pulls herself away from her darkness.

MANDA
I never did.

EDDIE
Snogged my face off. Got blood on your cheek, you snogged me so hard.

LISA
Can you stop it?

She finds a laugh.

MANDA
Maybe I did.

LISA
Why?

MANDA
Well. Your dad is really good at holding hands.

EDDIE gives MANDA's hand a squeeze.

He looks at LISA and then MANDA.

EDDIE
Shall we hold hands in Wainwrights?

LISA
No.

EDDIE
Little loved-up teenagers. Embarrassing our daughter.

LISA
I'm staying in the van.

EDDIE laughs again.

EDDIE
Come on. You child of love. You love-child. You child made of romance and petals. You child made of passion...

LISA
Shut up. Just shut up.

EDDIE gets out of the van grinning.

LISA smiles and follows him out.

MANDA follows them both. She notices LISA throw an embarrassed look back towards the van.

EXT. WAINWRIGHTS

They walk across the car park towards -

WAINWRIGHTS HARDWARE. A warehouse of a building. Clearly an institution.

EDDIE takes MANDA's hand.

LISA
No.

EDDIE swings MANDA's hand. MANDA laughs.

LISA (CONT'D)
No. No.

EDDIE laughs. They all laugh.

EDDIE
When I was a kid, these were the only places open on a Sunday you know? You might get a bric-a-brac market somewhere, or a car boot sale - but in terms of shops, you'd have your takeaways and your car shops - hardware stores was where the magic was for us kids.

LISA
They'd be the only place open?

MANDA
Sunday trading laws.

INT. WAINWRIGHTS

EDDIE, MANDA and LISA walk into the vast Wainwrights.

EDDIE
We used to go in and just wander about -

LISA
(to MANDA)
You too?

MANDA
No. I had church and Sunday lunch.

EDDIE
Your mother was a good girl. God knows how she turned out like she did...

MANDA
I got ruined – by someone.

EDDIE smiles. They walk further.

MANDA (CONT'D)
What exactly are we looking for?

EDDIE
I'll meet you by the tills.

MANDA
And what are we supposed to do? Hang out in cycling?

EDDIE
I'll see you in a bit. Enjoy your day out. Have a mooch.

MANDA laughs. She takes LISA by the arm. LISA disengages.

MANDA
'Not in here, Mum, I might know someone.'

LISA
Shut up.

We travel down the aisle after EDDIE.

He turns into a new aisle. He looks up at the aisle signs.

He stops a shop employee, TERRY.

EDDIE
Excuse me mate. Could you give me a hand?

TERRY turns to EDDIE.

EDDIE (CONT'D)
Someone put paint on my van.
I just wondered if you could give
some advice on how to get it off.

TERRY
Erm yeah. I'll try and help.

TERRY nods. He doesn't know the answer.

TERRY (CONT'D)
Quint? Quint.

QUINT, further down the shelves, turns.

TERRY (CONT'D)
Guy's a dictionary when it comes
to weird stuff.

EDDIE
I just want paint remover
or...Not that weird.

QUINT comes ambling over, he's in his mid-twenties but looks ten years older.

QUINT
Alright.

TERRY
Paint job on a van...Wants to
remove it.

QUINT
What kind of paint?

EDDIE
Spray I think.

QUINT
You tried water and soap?

TERRY walks away.

EDDIE
Yeah. Didn't touch it.

QUINT
How powerful is your hose?

EDDIE smiles.

EDDIE
Well I've not had any complaints from the missus, mate.

QUINT
Okay...You'll need to hose it. Then you need paint thinner - or strong alcohol - vodka'd do it - isopropanol better - and a microfibre towel -

EDDIE
A what?

QUINT laughs.

QUINT
We sell them. Follow me. Circular movements with the towel. Bit of prayer. Best you can do.

EDDIE isn't sure he likes QUINT.

EDDIE
Bit of prayer. Will it not take it off?

QUINT
You may have - you'll probably have a residue. If you want it all off - it's a respray job. What is it, a tag? Bloody kids.

EDDIE is thinking.

EDDIE
Can you take me to your blue paint...?

QUINT
If it's paint you probably want
it resprayed.

EDDIE
I haven't got the cash for that.
Can't afford it.

He reads QUINT's badge. QUINT slightly changes in his eyes.

EDDIE (CONT'D)
Quint. Am I saying that right?
Take me to paint. Doesn't matter
if it matches exactly, just want
the worst of it gone...

QUINT
Oh.

EDDIE
What?

QUINT
I just worked out who you are.

EDDIE says nothing.

QUINT (CONT'D)
Seen you on Facebook. Photos. You
know.

EDDIE hates this.

EDDIE
Yup. Can you show me where the
paint is?

QUINT
Yeah. Aisle three. I'll take you.

They walk. EDDIE doesn't want to be near QUINT any more. He hangs back.

QUINT (CONT'D)
Sorry. Didn't mean to embarrass you or anything.

EDDIE
No. You're alright, mate.

QUINT
I'm on your side. Your son's side. For what that's worth.

EDDIE
Are ya.

QUINT
He didn't do it. No way. I mean, even the stab wounds - where they said there were stab wounds - there's bone in the penetration spots. If you're making stuff up, at least make it anatomically possible I say.

EDDIE is dying from the inside out.

QUINT (CONT'D)
And I've seen pictures of her - which I don't like much -

Beat. QUINT looks at EDDIE.

EDDIE
I'm just here for paint.

QUINT
Sorry. Just saying you've got my support.

EDDIE
Okay.

QUINT
And more than me. There's cleverer than me looking into it.

QUINT looks at EDDIE. EDDIE sees he means it. He takes a step back.

QUINT (CONT'D)
You should get him a good lawyer is what I think. If you crowdfund it, there's a lot of us who'd get behind it.

QUINT nods and goes to get the paint off the shelf.

QUINT (CONT'D)
Here's your paint. Fill your boots, big man.

QUINT heads off. EDDIE follows after a beat.

EDDIE turns to see QUINT looking back from a good way down the next aisle. Careful to protect himself.

EDDIE controls himself.

He turns back towards the front of the shop.

He finds his way to the tills.

He stands in the queue.

LISA appears and sees him. She sidles up behind him.

LISA
You know, there are actually people here for a day out. I saw one man just sort of smiling to himself at inner tubes -

EDDIE says nothing. LISA was expecting a smile.

LISA (CONT'D)
Are you okay, Dad?

EDDIE nods.

EDDIE
I'm okay. Just - hungry now.

LISA
Oh I know. Black pudding...

She smiles. He doesn't. She's surprised by this.

They reach the front of the queue.

The man on the till recognises the two of them instantly. He runs up the paint.

EDDIE doesn't meet his eye.

TILL MAN
Thirty-four ninety-nine.

EDDIE swipes his phone for payment.

He walks away from the till and out the doors.

EXT. CAR PARK. WAINWRIGHTS

EDDIE walks across the Wainwrights car park.

LISA walks a step behind him. She knows he's not right.

MANDA hurries out to join them both.

MANDA
Well, that was lovely...

Beat.

MANDA (CONT'D)
I think a fella in tyres checked me out actually...

Beat.

MANDA (CONT'D)
Maybe Wainwrights is a good pick-up place for the single lady.

Beat.

MANDA (CONT'D)
I think I'm going to get
a mountain bike for my birthday.

Beat.

MANDA (CONT'D)
What?

And then EDDIE spots the two lads - FREDO and PAUL - lingering at the side of the car park on the grass verge.

Shit.

EDDIE
That's him, isn't it?

MANDA
Who?

EDDIE
They're following me. They're
taking the piss, aren't they?
Taking me for a twat.

EDDIE dumps the paint as he breaks into a run.

MANDA
Eddie!

They look up and see him. FREDO is putting his shoe back on.

EDDIE
Oi! OI!

He runs towards them.

LISA
DAD! What are - you?

MANDA
EDDIE! Eddie.

MANDA and LISA are bewildered – but don't follow.

EXT. GRASS TRACK

PAUL pedals fast away down the path as FREDO struggles to get his shoe on.

EDDIE is after them. He's fast.

He jumps on FREDO on the ground.

EDDIE wants to punch and kick FREDO, but he doesn't. Instead, his rage comes out in a torrent.

EDDIE
WHO ARE YOU? WHO ARE YOU? WHO ARE YOU TO WRITE THAT? WHO ARE YOU TO SAY FUCKING ANYTHING AT ALL? STANDING THERE. PLAYING MEN. FUCK YOU. YOU UNDERSTAND ME? FUCK YOU. LAUGHING AT ME. DON'T YOU DARE LAUGH AT ME.

He pulls him to his feet. He looks at him.

EDDIE (CONT'D)
Who do you think you are ey? Come on, big man. Take a shot.

And then he sees something in their eyes he wasn't expecting – fear.

He stands a moment, swaying with that.

EDDIE (CONT'D)
Fuck.

He stands a moment more. His rage still pulsating.

EDDIE (CONT'D)
DID YOU DO MY VAN?

They say nothing.

EDDIE (CONT'D)
Wankers.

He makes to hit them. But he pulls back. He lets go of FREDO, who runs away down the path.

He turns to walk away, before picking up FREDO's bike and launching it at him.

EDDIE (CONT'D)
Don't forget your bike!!

And we walk with him as he tries to digest what he did and what he meant to do.

EXT. CAR PARK. WAINWRIGHTS

EDDIE emerges back into the car park.

He looks at MANDA and LISA waiting by the van.

He picks up the paint from where he dropped it. He looks to see if the tin is dented.

It is. He goes into his van for a screwdriver.

He undoes the paint pot.

EDDIE
Excuse me, stand back.

His hands are shaking. MANDA pulls LISA out of the way.

EDDIE throws the paint liberally over the side of the van.

It splashes everywhere, including the passenger-side door.

A great splodge of blue.

The graffiti is now obscured, but the van is even more damaged. The words 'Miller Plumbing' have been ruined.

EDDIE throws the empty tin across the fence. MANDA stands with her shopping (a plant or similar).

EDDIE (CONT'D)
Come on, give me them. Get in the van.

EDDIE turns and looks at MANDA and something passes between them. She knows she can't touch him when he's like this, but she can remind him where he is.

They walk around the other side of the van.

MANDA leads LISA, who is unsure what to do.

They get into the van.

EDDIE (CONT'D)
Come on, shufty along.

SECURITY GUARD
OI!

A SECURITY GUARD approaches across the car park.

EDDIE turns and looks at him, his screwdriver still in his hand.

EDDIE
You wanna say summit, mate!? You want your go do ya?

The SECURITY GUARD steps back. He can see danger.

EDDIE (CONT'D)
Get back in the fucking shop!

SECURITY GUARD
You're on camera.

EDDIE
You and your fucking mate, weird twat!

From the doorway, QUINT is watching. EDDIE gets into the van.

INT. MILLER VAN

There's a great sludge of blue over one side of the window.

EDDIE starts the van.

EDDIE
Everyone belted in?

MANDA
Yes.

LISA
Yeah.

There's silence as EDDIE drives away.

They all three look in different directions. Spinning on everything they've heard and done.

We stay in the silence.

We look at all three of the faces.

We breathe in their sadness.

EDDIE just stays intent on the road.

He knows where he's gone. Self-loathing and rage intermingle.

MANDA stays intent on EDDIE, without looking at him...

...and LISA looking between them - truly fragile.

And then EDDIE's phone rings through the hands-free.

And he looks at the number on it.

He looks at MANDA, she's seen too. She nods.

He presses accept, the phone call comes through the van's speakers.

VOICE
This is a recorded message from - Jamie Miller - at Standling Secure Training Centre. This call is from a person currently in a secure training centre in England or Wales. All calls are logged and recorded and may be listened to by a member of the secure training centre staff. If you do not wish to accept this call, please hang up now.

There's a pause. None of them moves a muscle.

JAMIE (O.S.)
Hello?

EDDIE makes a real effort.

EDDIE
Hello Jamie lad.

JAMIE (O.S.)
Dad.

Beat. MANDA leans forward as if to say something and then pulls back.

JAMIE (O.S.) (CONT'D)
Just wanted to say happy birthday.

EDDIE
Right, I mean, thank you. It's kind of you to call.

JAMIE (O.S.)
Did you get my card?

EDDIE
Yeah. Did you draw it?

JAMIE (O.S.)
Yeah.

EDDIE
Thought you did. It was really good.

JAMIE (O.S.)
Yeah.

EDDIE
Forgot how much you loved drawing.

JAMIE (O.S.)
Yeah. I loved drawing.

Beat.

EDDIE
How's it going in there? Has it died down a bit - all the noise?

JAMIE (O.S.)
Yeah. The librarian's alright to me, and - I'm getting some bother in the yard but it's - okay.

EDDIE
Remember, if it gets too much you know what to do...

JAMIE (O.S.)
I know. I got people to talk to.

There's a silence. Neither quite knows how to fill it.

JAMIE (O.S.) (CONT'D)
What you doing with your day?

EDDIE
Good yeah, your mum's going to do me a nice breakfast -

JAMIE (O.S.)
You haven't had breakfast yet?

EDDIE
- and then we thought we'd go to the pictures and get a Chinese tonight.

JAMIE (O.S.)
Kung po king prawn.

EDDIE
You know my order.

JAMIE (O.S.)
You got any good presents?

EDDIE
We haven't done presents yet.

Beat.

JAMIE (O.S.)
I had breakfast three hours ago.

EDDIE
Lucky you.

Beat.

JAMIE (O.S.)
Dad...

The worry surges across EDDIE's face, he senses a tone in JAMIE's voice.

EDDIE
Yeah?

JAMIE (O.S.)
I know today is not the day for it - but - it's just happened, you know, and I -

Oh shit. EDDIE blanches. But he's a dad.

EDDIE
Pretend it's not my birthday, what's going on?

JAMIE (O.S.)
Yeah. Well, yeah. Well, with it all getting closer. I've been doing some thinking. And I've decided to change my plea.

Every part of EDDIE tightens. JAMIE waits for him to say anything.

JAMIE (O.S.) (CONT'D)
Dad, I'm sorry, but - I've decided to say guilty.

EDDIE can't say anything. MANDA can see it.

MANDA
Hiya, son. We're here too.

LISA
I'm here, Jamie.

JAMIE (O.S.)
What? Oh, hi.

We study EDDIE, as he attempts to digest everything that's happened today.

Everything that's happened this year.

He suddenly feels really fucking old.

MANDA
Food getting any better?

JAMIE (O.S.)
Yeah. I thought it was just me and Dad...

MANDA
No. I wrote to them about your intolerances, love.

JAMIE (O.S.)
Yeah. That's all okay.

LISA
And are you still in the gym all the time?

JAMIE (O.S.)
Only when I'm allowed.

LISA
Going to turn into a bodybuilder or something...

JAMIE (O.S.)
Not really.

Beat.

JAMIE (O.S.) (CONT'D)
I better go. There's other people waiting.

MANDA
Yeah?

JAMIE (O.S.)
I'll call you usual time end of the week, yeah?

MANDA
Perfect.

JAMIE (O.S.)
Dad?

EDDIE
Yeah.

JAMIE hesitates.

JAMIE (O.S.)
Sorry.

There's a long pause. That word reverberates.

JAMIE waits for more, but there is no more.

JAMIE (O.S.) (CONT'D)
Happy birthday.

EDDIE
Thanks lad. And thanks for ringing.

JAMIE hangs up.

There is profound silence through the van.

EDDIE says nothing, and then says something under his breath.

MANDA looks across at him.

LISA stares out of the window.

INT. VAN / EXT. MILLER HOUSE

They park up outside the house.

EDDIE
Get out this side.

EDDIE gets out of the van first.

He walks into the house, taking MANDA's shopping for her.

An elephant dragging his feet through mud.

MANDA and LISA are left.

MANDA looks at LISA, who looks back at MANDA. LISA's broken.

LISA
Is he going to be alright?

MANDA
He's alright. Come on.

LISA gets out of the van.

MANDA takes the keys out of the ignition, and gets out of the van.

She locks it all up.

She looks at the paint. She touches it, it's still wet.

The window opens on the other side of the road.

EILEEN
What happened?

MANDA says nothing.

EILEEN
Kids was it?

MANDA
Fuck off, Eileen.

MANDA walks into the house.

Inside, she sobs, muffling the sound with her coat.

She shuts the door behind her.

INT. HALLWAY. MILLER HOUSE

MANDA walks up the stairs, composing herself.

INT. EDDIE AND MANDA'S BEDROOM. MILLER HOUSE

EDDIE is looking at the seal of the window.

EDDIE
He hasn't sealed these windows properly, I should have done it myself. How much did he charge?

MANDA
Is that the shirt I got you?

EDDIE
Yeah.

MANDA
Looks lovely on you. You're not bad for fifty.

He stands a moment, swaying.

MANDA (CONT'D)
We don't have to go to the pictures.

EDDIE hates the thought of leaving the house again.

EDDIE
No, we'll go.

MANDA
(quickly)
Let's just leave it, okay?

EDDIE
We can go.

MANDA
It's okay.

EDDIE
Okay. Ta.

MANDA knows she needs to be brave.

MANDA
I - uh - I thought he sounded better than he did [before] -

EDDIE says nothing.

MANDA (CONT'D)
Our Jamie.

EDDIE
Yeah.

MANDA
Maybe making a - maybe deciding - has made it a little better, hey?

EDDIE says nothing.

MANDA (CONT'D)
You do need to - we do need to - you remember what Jenny said -

EDDIE
Yeah.

He stands really still. MANDA doesn't like what she's seeing.

EDDIE (CONT'D)
Yeah. Not trying not to - yeah. What'd she say? Block you. Like I'm a centre-back. Or...

MANDA
Why you being like this?

EDDIE
Being like what?

MANDA
You were the one in with him. I haven't ever even seen the tape.

EDDIE
Let's not do that again.

MANDA
That's becoming your catchphrase isn't it? 'Let's not do this, let's not do that again.'

EDDIE
The - me being in - you not being in - with him.

MANDA
That wasn't what I was saying.

EDDIE
So what are you saying?

MANDA
You saw the tape - I didn't.

EDDIE takes a beat.

MANDA (CONT'D)
This isn't you, okay? You're soft and - this isn't you. Threatening kids, wrecking your van -

EDDIE takes a long time.

MANDA (CONT'D)
I know you're angry, but him going guilty is probably for the best. And if you were honest you'd see that too.

EDDIE
I saw what I saw and I didn't wanna believe it. I kept thinking - yeah, maybe it's when they put different celebrities' heads on different people doing weird stuff. Know what I mean?

MANDA sits down. She studies her husband. He looks at her, vulnerable.

MANDA
Eddie. I've known you since you had bumfluff. We've got to survive this.

EDDIE
And what if we - can't.

MANDA nods.

MANDA
Jenny says -

EDDIE
Fuck Jenny.

Beat.

MANDA
He never left that room. He'd come home. Slam the door. Up the stairs. On the computer. I'd see the light on at one a.m. I'd knock and say 'Jamie, school tomorrow' and the light'd turn off but he never said nothing -

EDDIE
We couldn't do nothing about that. All the kids are like that, you know, they watch porn and all kinds of stuff. Look at the fella who popped up on my phone, that lad going on about how men should be men and how to treat women, I was only looking for something for the gym, wasn't I? You can't keep an eye on them all the time.

MANDA
And he'd shout sometimes - his tempers - but then I thought, you had them tempers -

EDDIE
Don't say that. I didn't give him that. Did I give him that?

MANDA
No.

EDDIE nods. So vulnerable.

MANDA (CONT'D)
But I do - I sometimes - I think - I sometimes think we should have stopped it.

EDDIE says nothing. It's huge. The space left by that statement. He can't fill that space.

MANDA (CONT'D)
Seen it - and stopped it.

EDDIE
Yeah but it's not our fault. We can't think like that. Remember what she said? We can't blame ourselves.

MANDA
We made him.

Beat. Those words have such power.

MANDA (CONT'D)
Didn't we?

EDDIE's brain is chewing with possibility. He talks quietly.

EDDIE
When I was a kid and I'd do something wrong, my dad would whack me or take the belt to me and say 'you little bastard' - and he'd hit me and hit me and hit me and all I wanted...all

I wanted...was to be better than that.

Beat. He looks at her, so vulnerable.

EDDIE (CONT'D)
Was I? Better?

MANDA
You tried to be.

EDDIE
I tried?

MANDA
We both did.

Beat.

EDDIE
I tried taking him to football, and he wasn't very good, and they'd just stick him in goal. He didn't want to go but I thought it'd toughen him up -

MANDA
Yeah. You thought he'd like it.

EDDIE
And I stood there, on the sidelines, with the other dads laughing at him when the goals went in, and he'd look at me, but I couldn't look back. I couldn't look at my own boy.

MANDA
He idolised you.

EDDIE
And then he gave that up and we took him to boxing and that lasted ten minutes and then - he did his art - sitting at the

table, and he was dead good wasn't he? And then he didn't want to do that and he wanted the computer so we got him the computer, and the keyboard and the headset and the desk, and he went upstairs and at first I tried to join in – play computer games with him – but I was working long days and not getting home until six or seven. And he'd shut the door and I thought – if that's what he wants, and at least we know where he is and that he's safe, not like when we were kids. And there's jobs in computers, so if he gets good at that, I thought we were doing the right thing, you know...

MANDA
I was home earlier and I did no better.

EDDIE
You were a good mum. You are a good mum.

MANDA
I was a good mum. You were a good dad. Great dad. Amazing mum. Perfect. But we made him.

EDDIE
My dad made this. So how did I make that?

Beat.

MANDA
We didn't know what he was going to do.

Beat. EDDIE looks at his wife.

MANDA (CONT'D)
And maybe that's why he wanted you there. Knew you wouldn't believe it. Thought you'd protect him.

Beat.

EDDIE
How could I have protected him?

MANDA
You couldn't.

Beat.

EDDIE
Should I have protected him?

MANDA
No.

EDDIE
Could we have done more?

MANDA
I - think it'd be good - if we accepted - that maybe we should have done. I think that'd be okay. For us. To think that.

Beat.

EDDIE
I still see that little boy. Bit gormless. Swinging on the monkey bars. Drawing a picture of a monster. Eating an ice cream and most of it goes up his nose.

MANDA
I still see him too. His little face.

EDDIE
That was yesterday.

MANDA
I know.

Beat.

EDDIE
He kept saying - I didn't do it - he kept saying it - and I was there, and I looked him in the eye, and he gave me his word and I believed him.

MANDA
I know.

EDDIE
But then they showed the video -

Beat. She stands and approaches him. She touches him in just the small of his back.

EDDIE (CONT'D)
I wish it had've been you.

Beat.

EDDIE (CONT'D)
You'd have done better.

Beat.

MANDA
No

EDDIE
Yeah, you would. You'd have done better.

Beat. Something changes in EDDIE's face.

LISA enters the room, and then walks right out.

MANDA
Lisa, you're okay. Come in, love. You're okay.

LISA walks into the room. She's wearing a new outfit. She looks quite glamorous.

EDDIE
You okay, love?

LISA
Yeah.

MANDA sits down and pats the bed beside her. LISA comes in and sits on the bed.

EDDIE knows he needs to say something.

EDDIE
You got changed.

LISA
Yeah.

EDDIE
You look nice. Is it new?

LISA
No. Just - I probably am just wearing it different. Combinations are everything, guys.

Beat.

LISA (CONT'D)
I thought - when else do I get to look a bit smart - my dad's birthday - you know? Is that the top Mum bought you?

EDDIE
Yeah.

MANDA
I should dress up too.

EDDIE
You look nice as you are.

There's a moment between them.

EDDIE (CONT'D)
Sorry love. Sorry Lisa love. For - for what I did at the shop - to those boys - to the van -

LISA
The van looks worse. Can't read the word though, so...

EDDIE
I'll get it resprayed.

LISA
Were they the ones done it?

EDDIE
You know 'em?

LISA
Yeah, they're dickheads to be honest with you -

EDDIE
Lisa, language. If they cause you trouble - after what I did -

LISA
Everyone causes me trouble, Dad.

MANDA looks at her.

LISA (CONT'D)
I'm Jamie's sister.

Beat. She doesn't look at either of them.

LISA (CONT'D)
But we're staying here. We're not moving.

MANDA
But we could though.

LISA
If we move, Mum, it'll be better for a bit, then someone'll find out something, and that something'll become everything, and then suddenly it'll be even worse than before. Besides, Jamie's ours. Isn't he?

EDDIE looks at his daughter with such love.

He sits on the bed beside the two of them.

There's silence for a while.

MANDA
We thought we'd leave the pictures.

LISA
Yeah. Can rent a film at home maybe?

EDDIE
That sounds good.

LISA
Find some popcorn.

MANDA
We've got popcorn somewhere.

EDDIE
And then we can order in Chinese.

MANDA
Oh yes.

EDDIE
Prawn crackers for everyone.

They all smile. Making the best of it.

MANDA
Right. Time for breakfast. That black pudding will be sprouting legs and walking soon.

LISA gets up and heads to the stairs.

LISA
I'll set the table.

EDDIE
I'll help ya.

MANDA
You're coming nowhere near, birthday boy.

She gets up and makes to leave the room after LISA. Then turns and kisses her husband on the cheek.

He smiles. Moved by everything LISA said.

EDDIE
How did we make her then...

MANDA
Same way we made him.

She exits.

Leaves EDDIE sat there.

And we stay with him.

He thinks.

He walks forward.

We travel with him, urging him to follow.

We watch EDDIE step into Jamie's room.

INT. JAMIE'S ROOM

EDDIE sits on Jamie's bed.

He takes out and flicks through pictures on his phone.

They're pictures of the family, but particularly of Jamie.

He zooms in on one of them, Jamie sat on his bed. Looking unhappy.

EDDIE changes position so as to sit exactly as JAMIE did, with one knee up.

He thinks. He looks at the picture. Looking for clues.

EDDIE sways backwards and forwards.

This massive rush of emotion comes out. He doesn't make a noise, but the emotion just pours out.

He's not just crying, he's in a silent scream.

There's a teddy laying against his pillow. He buries his face in it. He tucks the teddy in.

EDDIE
I'm sorry, son. I should've done better.

He sways backwards and forwards, utterly overwhelmed.

CREDITS.

A Netflix Series
ADOLESCENCE

Cast in order of appearance

DI Luke Bascombe	Ashley Walters
DS Misha Frank	Faye Marsay
Manda Miller	Christine Tremarco
Eddie Miller	Stephen Graham
Jamie Miller	Owen Cooper
Lisa Miller	Amélie Pease
Tonia Simpson	Anne Hornby
PC Jenkins	Connor Calland
Eileen	Bibi Iredale
Derek	Jon Furlong
Sgt Golding	Neil Bell
PC Grogan	Jay Johnson
Erica	Faye McKeever
Paulie Barlow	Mark Stanley
Katie	Emilia Holliday
Mrs Fenumore	Jo Hartley
Mr Garfield	Robbie O'Neill
Ryan	Kaine Davis
Tommy	Lewis Pemberton
Adam Bascombe	Amari Bacchus
Fredo	Austin Haynes
Mrs Bailey	Hannah Walters
Mr Hutchinson	Craig Cheetham
Tau	Adam Khan
Shaun	Charlie McSweeney
Jade	Fatima Bojang
Moray	Alfie Ward
Mr Malik	Faraz Ayub
Carla	Melissa Johns
Mr Curtis	Jonathon Ojinnaka
Georgie Elodie	Grace Walker
Billie	Amelia Minto
Briony Ariston	Erin Doherty
Charlie	Tajinder Singh Chana

Victor	Douglas Russell
Frank	Claudius Peters
Paul	Liam Hawkins-Finnegan
Terry	Kaya Moore
Quint	Joe Barber

Crew

Stunt Coordinators	Steph Carey
	Derek Lea
Stunt Performers	Paul Bailey
	Elliott Cooper
	George Harris
	Chris Morrison
	Donna Williams
Pod Van Coordinator	Paul Bailey
Production Designer	Adam Tomlinson
Costume Designer	Jessica Schofield
Make-up and Hair Designer	Sian Wilson
Line Producer	Desmond Hughes
1st Assistant Director	Sarah Lucas
Financial Controller	Gareth Jones
Casting Director	Shaheen Baig
Music by	Aaron May and David Ridley
Sound Mixers	Kiff McManus
	Rob Entwistle
Supervising Location Manager	Tom Bartram
Post Production Producer	Hannah Dunnell
Colourist	Dan Moran
Re-Recording Mixer	Jules Woods AMPS CAS
Supervising Sound Editor	James Drake
Script Supervisor	Carley Armstrong
Gaffer	Max Hodgkinson
Key Grip	Pat Gillespie
Production Manager	Kerri Burbidge
Production Coordinator	Emmett Barlow
Assistant Production Coordinator	Joseph Taylor

Production Secretaries	Timka Fryer Dilpreet Rall
Production Runners	Emily Mitchell Janine Lanek
Sustainability Coordinator	Sarah O'Mahony
Access Coordinator	Julie Fernandez
Production Coordinator for Warp Films	Harriet Williams
Clearances by	Reviewed and Cleared
Production Accountant	John Gillett
1st Assistant Accountant	Charlotte Durnian
Payroll Accountant	James Allitt
Cashier	Hannah Griffith
Assistant Post Accountant	Luca Walton-Ryan
Stills Photographer	Ben Blackall
Script Editor	Hannah Christophe
Script Associate	Mariella Johnson
Police Advisor	Charlie Banks
Legal Advisor	Mark Bagshaw
Forensic Psychology Advisor	Lucy Schoolbred
Child Psychologist	Dr Rachel Andrew
Casting Assistants	Layla Wolf-Zarpak Connor Williams Emma-Jane Purcell Leila Ali
Assistant to P. Barantini	Laura Vincent
Assistant to J. Johnson	Katie Price
Assistant to S. Graham and H. Walters	Daya Taak
Production Legal Services	Lee and Thompson LLP
Tax Credit Audit	Shipleys LLP
2nd Assistant Director	Charlotte Allen
Crowd 2nd Assistant Directors	Nikita Vint Eric J. Blakemore
3rd Assistant Director	Ash Spall
Floor 3rd Assistant Director	Becky Topping
Crowd 3rd Assistant Directors	Courtney Evans Elvedin Gredeji Ben Plummer

Floor Runners	Adam Lloyd Jones
	Will Romain
	Ali Campbell
	Henrietta Lockwood
	Ben Plummer
	Becky Topping
Crowd Runners	Oscar Lock
	Cassie Clarkson
	Tara Nicholson
Intimacy Coordinator	David Thackeray
Acting Coaches	Zoe Ford Burnett
	Alison Rashley
Chaperones	Matt Lightowler
	Sarah Phoenix
	Steve Rawnsley
	Diane Aspin
	Amanda Grant
	Sophie Cunningham
	Sarah Craggs
	Jackie Evans
Camera Operators	Matthew Lewis
	Lee David Brown
1st Assistant Camera	Sean Beasley
2nd Assistant Camera	Adam Farquharson
Camera Trainees	Divine Zaki
	Natasha Booluck
Drone Pilot	Aaron Cole
Aerial Camera Operator	James Davis
Digital Imaging Technicians	Dan Wilkinson-Cain
	Stuart Liam McConville
Support Technician	Francis Hughes
Video Assist Supervisor	Jon Shepley
Video Assist Operators	Ben Banayo
	Keith Scott
	Hannah Richards
	Izzy Brittle
	Scott McKee
1st Assistants Sound	Kyle Pickford
	Tom Pallant AMPS
	Ashley Sinani

Sound Maintenance	Joanna Barcik Chi Limpiroj
Sound Trainees	Hannah Bracegirdle Lewis Monckton
Assistant Costume Designers	Tracey Cliffe Suzanne Bolton
Costume Supervisor	William Maher
Crowd Costume Supervisors	Suzanne Bolton Olivia Martin-Quirk
Principle Costume Standbys	Olivia Martin-Quirk Lucy Archbould Anakin Telle Nakata Hannah Riley Kiera Harvey
Crowd Costume Standbys	Claire Lilley Lilly Makinson Michelle Cash Christina Marshall
Junior Costume Standbys	Hannah Riley Georgia Stevenson Charlie Oxley
Costume Trainees	Megan Dunne Izzy Chambers Khai Joyce Emma Spurling Sarah Rafferty
Hair and Make-up Supervisor	Clare Ramsey
Crowd Hair and Make-up Supervisor	Madlen Mierzwiak
Hair and Make-up Artists	Jodie Marie Spencer Jenny Martin
Crowd Hair and Make-up Artists	Jo Adams Fiona Lobo Cranston
Hair and Make-up Junior	Helena Smythe
Crowd Hair and Make-up Juniors	Abigail Turner Karimah Farag
Hair and Make-up Trainee	Bethany Louita
Crowd Hair and Make-up Trainee	Maddox Bryson
Rigging Gaffer	Joe McDonald
Best Boy	Chris Davis

Desk Operators	Martin Winton
	Graham Leesmith
	Olly Suckling
Electricians	Vasco De Souza
	Matt Jas
	Richard Haigh
	Michael Bonnar
Rigging Electricians	Tom Ellis
	David Dolton
	Gav Davis
	Toby Enejere
	Shaun Kane
	Charlie Stewart
	Harry Dodd
	Matt Glaz
	Patrick Szelag
	Andrew Llewellyn
Grips	Pete Muncey
	Ben Lowe
Best Boy Grip	Asher Blythen
Grip Assistants	Adam Scollen
	Sam Bridges
Tracking Vehicle Driver	Max Bickers
	Adam Cheetham
Location Manager	Sharon Wood
Assistant Location Manager	Anika Kohli
Unit Manager	Sam Gannie
Location Assistant	Millan Hart
Location Trainee	Sam Thornton
Location Marshalls	Tiarnan Meely
	Loui Goodinson
	Dylan Naylor
	Natalie Jackson
	Jenni Canning
	Ben Robinson
	Isobel Rawnsley
	Simmi Ryatt
	Edward Barker
	Fiona Valentine
	Katie Jones

	Sian Williams
	Calla Cox
	David Hinitt
Art Directors	Ian Tomlinson
	Jordan McHale
Assistant Art Director	Nicola Presland
Standby Art Director	Esther Pearce
Draughtsperson	Liz Simpson
Art Department Assistant	Charlotte Groves
Art Department Trainees	Maia Walters
	Neelam Majumder
Graphic Designer	Victor Simão
Graphics Assistant	Francesca Wood
Senior Production Buyer	Paul Tormey
Production Buyer	Annabelle Ward
Assistant Production Buyer	Ulla Bergerud
Petty Cash Buyer	Amrit Kaur
Property Master	Gareth Procter
Dressing Props	Mark Jones
	Jay Pales
	Guy Spandler
	Neil Smith
	Russell Lee
	Carl Jones
Standby Props	Helen Straw
	Georgia Ward
Action Vehicles by	Anglo American
Action Vehicle Drivers	Grahame Peat
	James Dixon
	Andy Gladwin
	Ian Bentley
	Alan Podmore
	Garry Wall
	Robert Sutton
Armourer	Jason Payne
Construction Manager	Glen Brown
Standby Carpenter	Tom Higgins
Carpenters	Alan Jones
	Bryan Pollard
	Dean Henderson

	Gary McCabe
	Graham Henderson
	Jonathan Duxbury
	Peter Rimmer
	Stephen Hernandez
Decorating and Scenic Painting	CR Décor
Lead Scenic	Chris Rodwell
Scenic Painters	Dean Bush
	Andrew Seth
	Janet Fountain
	Joseph Fountain
	Danny Longfellow
	Jamie Price
	Nicole Shaw
Studios and Production Offices by	Production Park
Studio GM	Scott Matthews
Head of Production Services	Richard Blair
Studio Manager	Sam Wilkinson
Health and Safety Advisor	Helena Hanson
Unit Medics	Harry Hall
	Pat Gilding
	Andy Short
	Tulsa Thomas
	Steve Pratten
Rigging by	HRC Rigging
SFX by	Rowley SFX
Catering by	The Bee and Dragon Catering Company
Chefs	Ryan Hanley
	Sam Alldrick
	Jack Woods
	Wayne Briers
	Darren Rowberry
	Toby Hull
	Nick Wilkinson
	Helen Hanley
	Emily Twigg
Traffic Management by	Think!
Facilities by	ADF
Facilities Captain	Gabby Savin
Base Man	Andrei Calmuschi

Transport Captain	Mandy Meigh
Unit Drivers	Alex Crowney
	Danny Meigh
	Andy Ibbitson
	Dale Kirk
	Lee Killeen
	Paul Thomson
	Graham Butterworth
Minibus Drivers	Mick Bagshaw
	Henry Hamilton
	Ged Bailey
	Neil Clegg
Post Production Coordinator	Gabrielė Fedaravičiūtė
Assembly Editor	Jasmin John
1st Assistant Editor	Esmé Hill
Assistant Editor	Luke Smith
Editorial Trainee	Bella Roberts
Music Supervisor	Mark Kirby
Choir Production Manager	Amy MacIlraith
Titles Designed by	Simão Studio
Picture Post by	Harbor
Online Editor	Richard Ellis
Conform Editor	Steve Knight
Picture Post Executive	Rachael Yates
DI Coordinator	Paul McCullough
Audio Post by	Splice
Dialogue Editor	Michele Woods
ADR Editor	Emma Butt
Sound Effects Editor	Raoul Brand
Foley Supervisor	Adam Méndez
Foley Mixers	Rob Davidson
	Adam Méndez
Foley Editors	Rob Davidson
	Jessica Watkins
Foley Artists	Oli Ferris
	Sue Harding
	Andrea King
Audio Post Executive	Lydia Thatcher
VFX by	Absolute
VFX Supervisor	David Simpson

VFX Executive Producer	Danny Duke
VFX Producer	Mariluz Noto
VFX Line Producer	Zijing Huo
VFX Production Coordinator	Sarah Vaughan
VFX Editors	Ana Nunes
	James O'Shea
Pipeline Developer	Ben Hawkyard
Compositing Supervisor	Sivaprakash Jeevanantham
Compositors	Kannan Selvam
	Mohanbabu Subramani
	Surya Manohar
	Vijay Ramalingam
	Srinivas Tirupati
	Ashok Kumar Aravind
	Alice Mitchell
	Prasanth Balaji
	Vikash Singh
	Vignesh Kumar
	Rajarajan Nagarajan
	Ramkumar Raju
	Kathir Pandy
Prep	Raja Viswanathan
	Berlin Thiyagarajan
	Gokulakrishnan Narayanan
	Pratheesh Ganesan
Roto	Sathish Kumar
	Vishwa Nagasamy
	Smith Immanuel
	Surendar Manohar
	Prithiviraj Arunachalam
	Mithun Ramesh
Matchmove	Sangeetha Vasanth
	Sreedhar Ragavan
	Sivakumar Ramasamy
Director of Photography	Matthew Lewis
Co-Executive Producers	Carina Sposato
	Niall Shamma
	Peter Balm

Co-Producer	Leo Martin
Executive Producers	Jack Thorne Philip Barantini Brad Pitt Jeremy Kleiner Dede Gardner Nina Wolarsky Hannah Walters Stephen Graham Mark Herbert Emily Feller
Written and Created by	Jack Thorne and Stephen Graham
Directed by	Philip Barantini
Produced by	Jo Johnson